ABOUT THE AUTHOR

Christopher Barnatt is a futurist, videographer and Associate Professor of Computing & Future Studies in Nottingham University Business School. He has written eight previous books and numerous articles on future studies and computing, appears regularly in the media, and runs the websites ExplainingTheFuture.com, ExplainingComputers.com and their associated YouTube channels. You can follow him at twitter.com/ChrisBarnatt.

By the same author:

BOOKS

Seven Ways to Fix the World
25 Things You Need to Know About the Future
A Brief Guide to Cloud Computing
Cyber Business: Mindsets for a Wired Age
Challenging Reality: In Search of the Future Organization
Valueware: Technology, Humanity and Organization
Management Strategy & Information Technology
The Computers in Business Blueprint

WEBSITES

ExplainingTheFuture.com
ExplainingComputers.com

YOUTUBE CHANNELS

YouTube.com/ExplainingTheFuture
YouTube.com/ExplainingComputers

3D PRINTING
THE NEXT INDUSTRIAL REVOLUTION

Christopher Barnatt

ExplainingTheFuture.com

First published by ExplainingTheFuture.com®

For press, rights, translation and other enquiries,
please e-mail chris@explainingthefuture.com

ISBN-10 : 1-484-18176-X

7/2014

ISBN-13 : 978-1-484-181768

Printed and bound on demand.

Typeset in Adobe InDesign by Christopher Barnatt.

Disclaimer

While every effort has been made to ensure that the content in
this book is as accurate as possible, no warranty or fitness
is implied. All trademarks included in this book are
appropriately capitalized and no attempt is made
or implied to supersede the rights of their
respective owners.

1 3 5 7 9 10 8 6 4 2

To Mum & Dad

CONTENTS

ACKNOWLEDGEMENTS

While writing this book I have spoken or electronically communicated with many 3D printing pioneers. I would therefore like to thank all of those kind people who have taken the time to be interviewed, or who have otherwise provided me with information. A terrific 'thank you' therefore goes to Andy Ide from 3dfuture.com.au, David Blundell from Replicator World, Mark Fleming from 3DPrinter.net, Aaron Holmes and Jessica Rosenkrantz from Nervous System, Jo Roach from MakieLab, Domenico Cafarchia from D-Shape, Alex Schmid from Fabforall.com, Anssi Mustonen from AMD-TEC, Reuben Menezes from Proto3000, Marc Levinson and Richart Ruddie from Protos Eyewear, John Keaton from ThatsMyFace.com, Bathsheba Grossman from Bathsheba Sculpture, Jenna Franklin from EnvisionTEC, Brook Drum from Printrbot, Tyler McNaney from Filabot, Adrian Bowyer from RepRapPro, Franz Achatz from ReprapUniverse.com, Miranda Bastijns from i.materialise and .MGX, Robert Liska from the Technical University of Vienna, Ibrahim Ozbolat from the Biomanufacturing Laboratory at the University of Iowa, and Mike Childs from Friends of the Earth. You will learn more about these people and their organizations later in this book.

More broadly I would like to thank Deborah Ritchie and Steve Upcraft for their long-standing support for my writing, and Steve Moore, Kieran Woodward, Chris Bates, Sally

Hopkinson, Victoria Wrigley and Rozina Shaikh for generally putting up with me wandering into their office to talk about all kinds of stuff. Thanks also to Stephen Diacon, Ken Starkey, Sue Tempest, George Kuk, Duncan Shaw, Thomas Chesney, Tracey Bettinson, Kathleen Visser and Sallie Kirk for suffering me over the last few months as I have written my ninth book.

Finally, a great many thanks to my parents and to my old friend Mark Daintree for their support, encouragement and understanding as I have undertaken another of these love-and-hate writing journeys. I do still claim that I will not do it again for some time. But you never know!

PREFACE

Many times across history a new technology has transformed our lives. Not least steam engines, assembly lines and personal computers all drove their own period of industrial transformation. Today, the latest revolution of the Internet is just about over, with developments in the online world settling into a gentle pattern of 'evolution'. Yet even as this is occurring, a new revolution is waiting in the wings.

This time the technology that is going to change things is called 'additive manufacturing' or '3D printing'. These terms both refer to a widening range of technologies that turn computer models into real, solid objects by building them up in a great many very thin layers. For nearly 30 years 3D printers have been used in some industries to create concept models, rapid prototypes or mold masters. But the application of the technology is now starting to widen, with more and more pioneers using 3D printers to manufacture final products or parts thereof.

Within a decade or so, it is likely that a fair proportion of our new possessions will be printed on demand in a local factory, in a retail outlet, or on a personal 3D printer in our own home. Some objects may also be stored and transported in a digital format, before being retrieved from the Internet just as music, video and apps are downloaded today. While the required technology to allow this to happen is still in its infancy, 3D printing is developing very rapidly indeed. Some people may tell you that 3D printing is currently being over-hyped and will have little impact on industrial practices and our personal lives. Yet these are the same kinds of individuals who once told us that the Internet was no more than a flash in the pan, that online shopping would have no impact on traditional retail, and that very few people would ever carry a phone in their pocket.

In 1939 the first TV sets to go on sale in the United States were showcased at the World Fair in New York. These early TVs cost between $200 and $600 (or about the same as an automobile), and had rather fuzzy, five inch, black-and-white screens. Most of those who attended the World Fair subsequently dismissed television as a fad that would never catch on. After all, how many people could reasonably be expected to spend a large proportion of their time staring at a tiny, flickering image?

The mistake made by those who dismissed television in 1939 was to judge a revolutionary technology on the basis of its earliest manifestation. Around 75 years later, those who claim 3D printing to be no more than hype are, I think, in danger of making exactly the same error. As we shall see in chapter 2, over a dozen 3D printing technologies have already been created, with most in successful commercial application. Even so, we ought not to judge the potential of 3D printing on the basis of even the best of today's hardware. A fantastic technological foundation has now certainly been laid, with current 3D printers already allowing pioneering individuals and organizations to achieve things in new ways. But this point made, one of the key messages of this book is the need for us to recognise current 3D printers as a critical if transitionary stepping-stone to the future hardware that will herald the dawn of the Next Industrial Revolution.

With the above in mind, the goal of this book is to help you understand the practicalities and potential of 3D printing today, and to try and foresee its impact on the world of tomorrow. Whether you are an entrepreneur, designer, investor, technology enthusiast, student, DIY practitioner, or simply fascinated by new things, my hope is that the following chapters will prepare you for the next round of radical technological change.

The beginning of any revolution is always its most exciting period. The people who partake in a revolution's early stages are also likely to be those who will reap the greatest rewards, leave the strongest legacy, and have the most fun. The 3D Printing Revolution really is just about to happen. It is therefore high time for all those with vision to get involved.

Christopher Barnatt,
May 2013.

1

THE NEXT REVOLUTION

As I emerged from Moorgate underground station it was starting to rain quite hard. Most of the area outside the station was also boarded up for building work, making it difficult to orientate myself with the crumpled Google Map hardcopy in my hand. Even so, I stepped out into the dull, damp early afternoon of 19th October 2012 with a spring in my step. I was on a mission. And it was going to be rather interesting.

Arriving anywhere in a city around 1:00pm is never ideal, and especially so when it is raining and those on their lunch break are intent on using umbrellas to stop non-locals finding their way. Nevertheless I persisted, and was soon arriving at a venue called The Brewery.

As I crossed its cobbled courtyard I realized that The Brewery was a very upmarket place indeed. Well before the main entrance I was intercepted by an immaculately dressed young man with an extremely large umbrella. For a second I thought my clothing choice of a leather jacket had let me down and I was about to be turned away. But no, the now soggy ticket I was clutching along with my Google Map was enough to assure him I was legit, and I was let through.

On the door I was asked whether I was 'trade or press?' My answer of 'both really' did not phase an equally immaculately attired doorman, and I joined a short queue at a registration desk. A moment later my bedraggled ticket was exchanged for a glossy programme, and a plastic purple bracelet had been secured around my left wrist.

The strap line on the programme proclaimed that the Internet had changed the world in the 1990s, and that the world was about to change again. With this statement I also agreed. I had just arrived at the 2012 3D Printshow – the first major 3D printing event to be held in the United Kingdom, and one of the first in the world.

I was there in part to shoot a video, and so before I left the registration desk I asked if there were any restrictions on the use of cameras. They knew of none, and suggested that I visit their gallery of 3D printed works of art as the main exhibition halls were yet to open.

The gallery was down several flights of red-carpeted stairs, and entering it was a bit like stepping into another world. The room was already heaving with people, and most were looking at its 3D printed exhibits through the cameras on their smartphones or iPads. Clearly my question about what could be photographed had been irrelevant! The room was also liberally festooned with things worth committing to flash memory.

3D printers turn digital computer models into solid, physical objects by building them up in a great many very thin layers. As the exhibits in the art gallery demonstrated, already objects can be 3D printed in a wide range of materials including plastics, metals and ceramics. At the centre of the room were a pair of white, high-fashion 3D printed shoes that their designer told me would be worn on the catwalk that evening. Only one plinth away was a display of very colourful 3D printed vases. Next to them were some intricate 3D printed metal sculptures, including one in the shape of a teapot. Elsewhere in the room were a 3D printed iPhone case, all kinds of jewelry, a fragmented human head 3D printed in black plastic, and a computer keyboard with raised 3D printed keys in the shape of a city skyline.

Many of those milling around in the gallery were clearly amazed that everything on display had been 3D printed. Yet this was just the beginning of a very eye-opening three day event. Upstairs in the main exhibition halls we were all soon to see scores of functioning 3D printers, as well as a plethora of their creations. These included coffee cups, several lampshades, two guitars, a bikini, a range of customized dolls, a fabulous model of a concept car, two prosthetic limbs, a hoard of plastic robots, and an Egyptian mummy 3D printed from a digital scan. Figure 1.1 illustrates some of the many 3D printed objects that were on display.

In addition to hundreds of fascinating exhibits, the 3D Printshow also harboured a very noticeable buzz. As I toured the exhibition halls and talked to both exhibitors and fellow attendees, it was incredibly obvious that something very significant was starting to happen and that we were all part of a watershed event. From the conversations taking place it was also clear that many visitors were in attendance because they planned to become the entrepreneurs, scientists, artists or investors who would help shape the Next Industrial Revolution.

SO HOW DOES 3D PRINTING WORK?

OK, I have hopefully now captured your attention! But how, you may be wondering, does the apparent magic of 3D printing actually work? Well, to a large extent, the processes involved are no more than a logical evolution of the 2D printing technologies currently in use in a great many offices and homes.

Most people are familiar with the inkjet or laser printers that produce most of today's documents or photographs.

These create text or images by controlling the placement of ink or toner on the surface of a piece of paper. In a similar fashion, 3D printers manufacture objects by controlling the placement and adhesion of a 'build material' in 3D space.

To 3D print an object, a digital model first needs to exist in a computer. This may be fashioned by hand using a computer aided design (CAD) application, or some other variety of 3D modelling software. Alternatively, a digital model may be created by scanning a real object with a 3D scanner, or perhaps by taking a scan of something and then tweaking it with software tools.

However the digital model is created, once it is ready to be fabricated some additional computer software needs to slice it up into a great many cross sectional layers only a fraction of a millimetre thick. These object layers can then be sent to a 3D printer that will print them out, one on top of the other, until they are built up into a complete 3D printed object.

Exactly how a 3D printer outputs an object one thin layer at a time depends on the particular technology on which it is based. As we shall see in chapter 2, already there are more than a dozen viable 3D printing technologies. This said, almost all of them work in one of three basic ways.

Firstly, there are 3D printers that create objects by extruding a molten or otherwise semi-liquid material from a print head nozzle. Most commonly this involves extruding a continuous stream of hot thermoplastic that very rapidly sets after it has left the print head. Other extrusion-based 3D printers manufacture objects by outputting a molten metal, or by extruding chocolate, cheese or cake frosting (icing sugar) to 3D print culinary creations. There are even experimental 3D printers that output a computer-controlled flow of liquid concrete, and which may in the future allow whole buildings to be 3D printed.

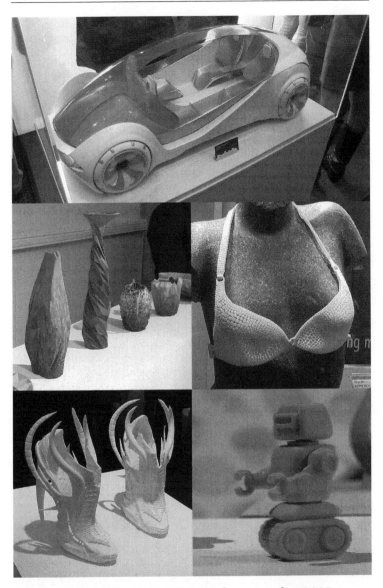

Figure 1.1: Exhibits at the 3D Printshow, London 2012.
'Ula Miami' car by Josh Henry and Materialise. 'Digital Natives' vases
by Matthew Plummer Fernandez. 'N12' bikini by Continuum Fashion.
'Exoskeleton' shoes by Janina Alleyne. Tiny robot by 3D Systems.

A second category of 3D printer creates object layers by selectively solidifying a liquid – known as a 'photopolymer' – that hardens when exposed to a laser or other light source. Some such 'photopolymerization' 3D printers build object layers within a tank of liquid photopolymer. Meanwhile others jet out a single layer of liquid and then use an ultraviolet light to set it solid before the next layer is printed. A few of the 3D printers that are based on the latter technology are able to mix and solidify many different photopolymers at the same time, so allowing them to print out multi-material objects made of parts with different material properties. For example, the latest Connex printers from a company called Stratasys can build objects in up to 14 different materials at the same time. These range from hard plastics in a range of transparencies and colours, to softer, rubber-like compounds.

A final category of 3D printing hardware creates objects by selectively sticking together successive layers of a very fine powder. Such 'granular materials binding' can be achieved either by jetting a liquid glue or 'binder' onto each powder layer, or by fusing powder granules together using a laser or other heat source. Already granular materials binding can be used to 3D print objects in a very wide range of materials. These include nylon, ceramics, wax, bronze, stainless steel, cobalt chrome and titanium.

WHY 3D PRINT?

Like any new development, 3D printing will only drive a revolution if it can offer clear and significant benefits over existing technologies and industrial practices. Before we proceed any further, it is therefore worth outlining how 3D printing may help us to usefully achieve new things, or else to achieve old things in more effective ways.

IMPROVING PRODUCT DESIGN

Already 3D printing is starting to be used to improve product design. It does this by facilitating the rapid creation of 'concept models', so allowing physical manifestations of in-progress designs to be viewed and handled early in the design process.

While computer graphic renderings of new products are now highly sophisticated, still nothing compares to holding a 3D model of a potential new product in your hand. Often potential design flaws that are not obvious when a design is viewed on a computer screen or tablet become very evident when a physical concept model can be seen and touched. By allowing concept models to be rapidly created – sometimes in full colour – 3D printers are therefore already improving the communication flow between designers and their clients. In turn this often helps to speed up the design process, as well as allowing better products to be created.

Beyond the concept design stage, 3D printers are also already being used to create 'verification models' or 'functional prototypes'. For this reason, in some industrial circles 3D printing has subsequently become known as 'rapid prototyping' or 'RP'. This is also a little sad, as in my experience the use of the 'rapid prototyping' label is blinding some people to the wider application of 3D printing technology.

Functional prototypes need to be created during most design processes to check the form, fit and function of a product's different parts. Traditionally such prototypes could only be created by skilled craftspeople using labour-intensive workshop techniques. It was therefore not uncommon for many product prototypes to take many weeks to produce and to cost thousands or tens of thousands of dollars, pounds euro or yen. In contrast, 3D printers can now often produce functional prototypes in a few hours for a tiny fraction of the price of traditional methods. The use of 3D printing is therefore already making prototyping quicker and cheaper, and in turn allowing new products to cycle through more iterations. As just one example, since 1998 the Renault Formula 1 racing team has been using 3D printers to produce prototype car parts to test the aerodynamic properties of its new designs. This allows the team to test hundreds of possible aerodynamic changes to its Formula 1 cars every year.

Over the past couple of decades, several 3D printing pioneers have set up successful businesses that specialize in producing concept models and functional prototypes. Many such companies are today continuing to thrive. But the falling cost of 3D printer hardware is also starting to allow many of their clients to move concept model and prototype production in-house, and even onto the desktop. Some Ford engineers, for example, were recently reported to be using 'MakerBot' desktop 3D printers that cost a few thousand dollars. These allow the creation of plastic components that can be assembled to check fit and function. The use of 3D printers by Ford engineers is hence helping to 'bridge the gap between the abstract and the practical' in new engine development.

TRANSFORMING TRADITIONAL PRODUCTION

Beyond concept model and prototype fabrication, 3D printers are also starting to be used in industrial pre-production. Most traditional production processes require the creation of bespoke jigs, tools, patterns and molds that are then used during manufacturing to shape metals and plastics into appropriate forms. Like product prototypes, such items have traditionally been crafted by hand in a manner that has proven both time consuming and expensive. The use of 3D printers to help tool-up factories for traditional production may therefore save a great deal of time and money.

A particularly promising application of 3D printing is in the direct production of molds, or else of master 'patterns' from which final molds can be taken. For example, as we shall see in the next chapter, '3D sand casting' is increasingly being used to print molds into which molten metals are then directly poured to create final components. As explained by ExOne – a pioneer in the manufacture of 3D printers for this purpose – by 3D printing sand casting molds, total production time can be reduced by 70 per cent, with a greater accuracy achieved and more intricate molds created. In fact, using 3D sand casting, single part molds can be formed that would be impossible to make by packing sand around a pattern object that would then need to be removed before the mold was filled with molten metal.

Some 3D printer models are created exclusively for the production of molds or patterns. For example, the range of Solidscape printers sold by a company called Stratasys print in wax-like plastics that are used to produce small molds or patterns in dental labs or for jewelry making. Like sand casts, these molds or patterns are 'sacrificial', as the process of producing a final object using them results in their destruction.

The use of 3D printers to create molds, patterns and other production tooling may rarely if ever be seen let alone appreciated by the consumers of most final products. For example, few people today are ever likely to realize that the soles of their trainers were probably produced in a mold that was derived from a 3D printed pattern master. Nevertheless, even though it will remain a behind-the-scenes development, the use of 3D printers in industrial pre-production is likely to prove a key facet of the 3D Printing Revolution.

DIRECT DIGITAL MANUFACTURING

While 3D printing is already an established part of some design and pre-production processes, the ultimate application of the technology will be in the development of 'direct digital manufacturing' (DDM). This does what it says on the tin, with DDM using 3D printers to create final products, or more usually parts thereof. As we shall see in chapter 4, DDM is already gaining traction in industries as diverse as aerospace, jewelry making, dentistry, toy production, and the manufacture of fashion items like designer homewares and customized sunglasses.

One of the amazing things about 3D printing is that it can be used to create objects which cannot be directly produced using traditional manufacturing techniques. For example, a 3D printer can print a necklace made up of links that do not have a break in them, not to mention a whistle with the pea already inside, or a ship in a bottle. Some 3D printers can also directly print working, multi-part mechanisms like gearboxes. Traditionally, the manufacture of multi-component products has always involved a final assembly stage. But when things are made using 3D printers this no longer has to remain the case.

In the future it is possible that almost anything could be manufactured using 3D printing technology, including entire aeroplanes. While this may sound crazy, a small team at Airbus is already designing a revolutionary airliner that would be 65 per cent lighter than a conventional aircraft because it would be 3D printed from a plastic resin. While such an aircraft – and the 3D printer required to make it – may not be ready until 2050, in 2011 Airbus parent company EADS opened a £2.6 million Centre for Additive Manufacturing at the University of Exeter. The goal of this research facility is to develop 3D printed parts for aircraft, including the current Airbus A380.

MASS CUSTOMIZATION

One of the key benefits of DDM is the ability to achieve mass customization, as no two objects produced on a 3D printer ever have to be the same. Some 3D printing pioneers have also begun to spot niche markets in which mass customization can allow totally novel products to be created. For example, visit Cubify.com, and you can create a custom iPhone case that will be 3D printed with a raised design on the back based on a digital image that you supply. In a similar fashion, ThatsMyFace.com invites visitors to upload a front and side photograph of their face, from which it then generates a coloured 3D model. ThatsMyFace customers can then have a 3D printed version of their head added to a selection of plastic action figures or a Lego model. Alternatively, they can purchase their face as a 3D printed portrait or mask.

The way in which ThatsMyFace.com purchases standard figurines, discards their heads, and replaces them with custom 3D printed parts, really is very clever indeed. The service not only allows anybody to own themselves in miniature super hero format, but more significantly demonstrates the potential to easily mass customize standard products using relatively low-cost 3D printing technology. For those seeking to create a new 3D printing business, similar opportunities across a great many other market sectors have to be considerable.

SMALL PRODUCTION RUNS

In addition to mass customization, DDM already allows one-off products or small batches of components to be produced at low cost, as no tooling is required to initiate production. For example, when the producers of the 2012 James Bond film *Skyfall* needed three 1/3rd scale models of an Aston Martin DB5, they had them 3D printed using a Voxeljet VX4000 3D printer. The replica cars were 3D printed in 18 parts that were then assembled and painted to be intensely accurate replicas of the real and far more expensive vehicle. Sadly the models were blown to smithereens during filming – although this was the reason that they were created in the first place.

As another example, a custom motorcycle manufacturer called Klock Werks Kustom Cycles has adopted 3D printing technologies to allow it to rapidly create one-off components. For one build, the company had just five days to produce a custom motorcycle to take part in a TV programme. To achieve this timescale, Klock Werk's engineers designed the bike's gauge pod, fork tube covers, headlight bezel, floorboard mounts, floorboard undercovers and wheel spacer cover in a 3D modelling package called SolidWorks. They then 3D printed the parts, rather than machining them from aluminium or injecting molding them in plastic. Their finished bike even went on to set an American Motorcyclist Association land speed record.

As the above high profile examples demonstrate, 3D printing is already being used to allow things to be created that simply could not be made as quickly or cheaply using traditional production methods. For companies – or indeed individuals – who wish to manufacture a single product or a small batch thereof, 3D printing is therefore already a technology that is making the impossible possible.

DIGITAL STORAGE & TRANSPORTATION

As well as enabling mass customization and small-scale manufacturing, 3D printing is set to facilitate digital object storage and digital object transportation. What this means is that, if you want to send something to somebody far away, in the future you will have two options available. The first will be to despatch the physical item via courier or mail, while the second will be to send a digital file over the Internet for 3D printout at the recipient's location.

While the above may sound like pure science fiction, already an object-sharing website called Thingiverse allows designers to upload digital creations that others can download for printout. Many people now regularly share text, photos and video online, and – due to 3D printing – digital objects are soon likely to be added to many social media collections. By making possible online storage and transportation, 3D printing is therefore set to do for physical things what computers and the Internet have already done for the storage and communication of digital information.

OPEN DESIGN

Possibilities will also increasingly exist for digital objects to iteratively evolve. Even today it is not uncommon for 3D printing enthusiasts to download a digital object, make an alteration or few, print the object out, and also re-upload their amended design so that others can benefit from the modifications they have made. So termed 'open design' is therefore starting to take hold, with more and more people having access to CAD software and 3D printer hardware that is democratizing the design process out of the hands of a privileged few.

While many firms fear the consequences of open design, others are strongly embracing the trend. For example, on 18th January 2013, Nokia launched a 3D printing community project. This included the release of a '3D printing development kit' to help people design and personally fabricate their own cases for its Lumia 820 phones. As explained by John Kneeland, a Community & Developer Marketing Manager at Nokia:

> Our Lumia 820 has a removable shell that users can replace with Nokia-made shells in different colors, special ruggedized shells with extra shock and dust protection, and shells that add wireless charging capabilities found in the high-end Lumia 920 to the mid-range 820.

Those are fantastic cases, and a great option for the vast majority of Nokia's Lumia 820 customers. But in addition to that, we are going to release 3D templates, case specs, recommended materials and best practices – everything someone versed in 3D printing needs to print their own custom Lumia 820 case.

Only a few days after Nokia make the above announcement it launched the Nokia Lumia 820 3D Printing Challenge to encourage people to design and share 3D printable replacement phone shells. By January 24th – only six days after the 3D printing development kit had been released – 3D printed Nokia 820 shells (including some with functional buttons) were being showcased on the web.

The above kind of practice may raise all sorts of intellectual property concerns. There are indeed already people who fear that 3D printing could wreak havoc with the functioning of capitalism itself by moving the means of production into individual hands.

Today 3D printing enthusiasts tend to share and iterate designs for objects such as smartphone cases, photographic accessories, toys and model vehicles. But there is no reason why parts and designs for pretty much anything could not be freely shared and iterated online. To the dismay of many, already people have managed to 3D print guns and share their designs. I will return to the wide-ranging issues that surround digital object replication, personal fabrication and open design in chapters 5 and 8.

TRANSFORMING RETAIL

While those who choose to own a 3D printer may increasingly fabricate their own objects at home, the mainstream impact of the 3D Printing Revolution is more likely to be felt in traditional retail locations. Today, all physical stores only have the space to stock a relatively small range of largely non-customized goods. They are also dependent on suppliers getting goods to them on time. However, by the end of the decade, at least some retailers may have installed high-end 3D printers that will allow them to print-on-demand customized goods from a potentially unbounded digital object inventory that will never go out of stock. It also clearly makes sense both environmentally and financially for most people to 'share' large 3D printers that reside in retail locations, rather than for everybody to own the latest personal fabrication hardware.

To serve the needs of those who want to design their own products, but who do not want or cannot afford to own a personal 3D printer, 3D printing bureaus are additionally likely to become big business. As already mentioned, companies that offer industrial rapid prototyping services have existed for many years. But alongside them we are now starting to see the rise of both online services and physical stores that are intent on bringing 3D printing to the masses.

For example, if you happen to be in Los Angeles, you can call in to The Buildshop at 201 North Westmoreland Avenue to design and 3D print your own stuff. Or regardless of where you live, browse-on-over to i.materialise.com and you can upload your own designs and get them 3D printed in a choice of over 20 materials. Via the i.materialise gallery, you can also make your designs available for online sale to others. Already this kind of service is removing the barriers to entry in some industries, as anybody can now design and sell physical things without having to invest in any stock or tooling whatsoever, as every item sold is 3D printed on demand. Right now, freelance artists and jewelry makers are some of the largest users of online 3D printing services. But they are not going to remain the majority customers in the print-on-demand marketspace for very long.

IMPROVING HUMAN HEALTH

Today, while most things that are 3D printed are made from plastics or metals, already there are specialist 3D printers that can build up living tissue by laying down layer-after-layer of living cells. Such 'bioprinters' have the potential to transform many areas of medicine by allowing replacement skin and human organs to be 3D printed from a culture of a patient's own cells. If this happens – and bioprinting pioneers expect that it will within two decades – then the development of 3D printing may cut organ donor waiting lists to zero, as well as making skin grafts a thing of the past. In as little as five years, 3D printed tissues may also start to be used in drug testing, so lessening the requirement for animal experimentation.

In addition to 3D printing replacement human tissues outside of the body, *in vivo* bioprinting is already in development. This involves 3D printing layers of cultured cells directly onto a wound, or even inside the body using keyhole surgery techniques. Should this kind of technology become advanced enough, one day instruments may be able to be inserted into a patient that will remove damaged cells and replace them with new ones. Such instruments may even be able to repair the wound created by their own insertion on their way out. While such hypothesis may sound fantastical, some medical practitioners and 3D printing pioneers are already taking them very seriously indeed. I will discuss bioprinting in depth in chapter 7.

SAVING THE PLANET

The final and potentially the most significant benefits of 3D printing may turn out to be environmental. Today, vast quantities of oil and other resources are used to move products around the planet, with a great many things travelling hundreds or thousands of miles before they come into our possession. Given the increasing pressure on natural resource supplies – not to mention probable measures to try and combat climate change – within a decade or two such mass transportation may be neither feasible nor culturally acceptable. Local fabrication-on-demand could therefore turn out to be 3D printing's long-term killer advantage.

In addition to facilitating digital object transportation, 3D printing is also potentially far more environmentally friendly than many forms of traditional industrial production. This is simply because it is based on 'additive manufacturing'. In other words, while many traditional production techniques start with a block of material and cut, lathe, file, drill or otherwise remove bits from it in a subtractive fashion, 3D printing starts with nothing and adds only the material that the final object requires. Digital manufacturing using 3D printers can therefore result in substantial raw material savings.

When final product parts are 3D printed, manufacturers can also optimise their designs so that each part consumes the minimum of materials. 3D printed plastic or metal parts can, for example, be designed with internal air gaps or open lattice work that cannot be fabricated inside an object produced using traditional production techniques. Such a design approach also allows lighter parts to be created – a manufacturing opportunity that the aerospace industry is very keen to take forward.

As a final environmental benefit, 3D printers may find significant application in the production of spare parts. Today, when most things break they cannot be mended as spares are simply not available. But with more and more 3D printers on hand, the opportunity will soon exist to fabricate whatever parts are needed to mend a great many broken things.

Today, most of us still embrace a culture of mass disposability that favours the consignment of broken possessions to landfill rather than regular product repair. Yet as natural resources dwindle, over the next few decades attitudes and practices will have to change. At least in part, it may also turn out to be 3D printing that facilitates our return to a society in which we increasingly opt to repair rather than replace. I will explore the actual and potential links between 3D printing and sustainability in chapter 6.

CATALYSTS FOR A REVOLUTION

So far in this chapter I have provided a brief overview of what 3D printing is, a quick run-through of how it works, and a summary of its current and potential future advantages. In doing so I have hopefully convinced you that a 3D Printing Revolution really is now on the cards. This said, given that 3D printing has been around for several decades, you may reasonably be asking why the 3D Printing Revolution has not happened in the past, and just why it is about to take off right now.

The answer to the above key question is inevitably multifaceted. For a start, 3D printing has had to wait for the substantial improvements in computer processing power, storage and network infrastructure that now potentially allow almost anybody to create, exchange and generally work with digital 3D objects. When first generation 3D printers came onto the market in the late 1980s and early 1990s, the industrial PC workstations used for 3D object design were expensive, and the idea of exchanging large quantities of data over the Internet was ludicrous. Yet today, many smartphones and tablets – let alone desktop PCs and laptops – are powerful enough to be used to design and store complex 3D objects. A high speed Internet is now also a reality, in turn meaning that the online storage and communication of 3D objects no longer presents a technical challenge. As if to demonstrate how far we have come, some of the personal 3D printers being showcased at the 2012 3D Printshow were wirelessly connected to iPads.

Technological advances made in the world of 2D printing have also helped to build the foundations of the 3D Printing Revolution. While 3D printers are by no means the same as their 2D ancestors, most do rely on somewhat similar servo motors and feed mechanisms, lasers, inkjet print heads, and electronic controllers. The advancement of such hardware over the past two decades was hence a necessary prerequisite to a printing revolution of the 3D kind.

In a bizarre kind of way, the development of 3D printing has also had to wait for the development of 3D printing itself. Here I am referring to the fact that some developments in low-cost 3D printer hardware have relied on the efforts of enthusiasts who have used early 3D printers to help innovate and build better models. Open source 3D printers called 'RepRaps' were in fact always intended to be 'replicating rapid prototypers' capable of partially reproducing themselves in order to facilitate the creation of next generation machines. In a sense, and as we shall see in chapter 5, at a grassroots level 3D printing is therefore quite literally a technology that has taken some time to almost organically evolve.

A fourth factor that is catalyzing the 3D Printing Revolution right now is the increasing digitization of human activity. Even ten years ago, most people rarely if ever went online, with very few of us communicating digitally or harbouring digital possessions. In stark contrast, today billions of people use the Internet, while owning a digital music, photo or video collection is hardly unusual. The idea of using 3D printers to fabricate physical objects from online digital data is therefore far more likely to be enthusiastically embraced right now than it was when 3D printers were first invented.

Finally, some of the patents on 3D printing technology that were taken out in the late 1980s and early 1990s have either run out, or will soon expire. Some of the potential legal barriers that may until now have slowed the 3D Printing Revolution are therefore starting to fall.

IN THE WORDS OF PIONEERS

The 3D Printing Revolution is – like any other – the product of the actions, energies and visions of those pioneers who are brave enough to make it happen. Throughout this book I will report on what such pioneers are doing, and will also include extracts of my original interviews with some of those who are driving things forward. Right now, in this chapter, my goal is to capture your imagination rather than to focus on details and practicalities (we do, after all, have the rest of the book for that). So, as we head toward the end of this introduction, I thought I would report the responses of a few 3D printing pioneers when I asked them the fundamental question 'why 3D print?'

One of the first people I spoke to was Alex Schmid, who runs the 3D printing search engine Fabforall.com. As he enthused:

> We think that 3D printing matters in the same way that the Internet matters to people and businesses. It means an amazing explosion of creativity, personal enabling, global connectivity [and] disruptive innovation in the material world [to match what] the Internet did in the digital realm.

Reuben Menezes works for Proto3000, a company that provides 3D printing and related product development services in North America. As he argued:

> From my perspective, there are really two parts to this 3D printing journey. The first being the consumer. I believe that 3D printers in the hands of consumers will mean the end of standardization, and the beginning of products personalized to every individual. The second portion of this 3D printing paradigm is its effect on manufacturing and production. Already, 3D printed parts are being used as end-products, achieving new levels of cost-reduction. Not to mention, on the horizon are new 3D printing materials with properties that rival existing elements. [For example] in a few years plastics could rival the strength of metals through the use of nano-technology in 3D printing.

Miranda Bastijns is Director of the Belgium-based 3D printing services i.materialise and .MGX. As she explained:

> 3D printing helps create a world where the products we buy have a better fit, a better match to one's personal style, and where we all have the ability to own something that is truly unique.
>
> For consumers, it is exciting that individuals can now not only create products that better serve their own needs and interests, but also start to sell the result to others like them. For example, a jewelry designer can offer their latest ring to a global audience and test the demand for the design. If there are no orders, no problem – and if there are, then the

rings will be printed, delivered to the customer, and the designer will receive their share of the profit.

Anssi Mustonen, who runs AMD-TEC, a 3D printing and design company in Finland, focused on the customer service angle:

> We live in a hectic world and for me 3D printing is almost the only way to serve my clients as well as I can. For prototyping I don't have time to program [CNC machines] and I don't have time to send quotations to machining companies to get parts. 3D printing is not the only way to make parts, but it's faster when creating complex shapes and configurations than [using] traditional methods.

David Blundell, the writer and editor of *Replicator World*, brought a range of arguments together in signalling the truly revolutionary potential of 3D printing. As he enthused:

> The 3D Printing Revolution marries the rapid production of the Industrial Revolution with the global distribution of the Digital Revolution. For two hundred years, mass production has shackled the individualization of products. As Ford once said of his Model T, 'you can have any color you want, as long as it's black!' But with the ascension of 3D printing the means of production have begun to move to the desktop. You can truly now have any color you want. Or shape. Or function. All over the world millions of tiny personal factories creating personal products are springing up. Objects designed for the people by the people. Welcome to the future.

I could go on to cite a great many more pioneers who believe that the 3D Printing Revolution is both about to happen and will yield great benefits. Though hopefully from the above five quotations you have garnered the impression that I am far from alone in proposing that a step-change is now set to occur in how we manufacture quite a few things. The words of Alex, Reuben, Miranda, Anssi and David have also I trust served to demonstrate the sheer energy and passion of those who are driving our next wave of radical change.

THE PC OF CENTURY 21

In 1943 Thomas Watson, the founder of IBM, reputedly stated that there would be 'a world market for about five computers'. If this is what he actually said, then to date he has been caught out by a factor of at least a billion. And even if it is not exactly what he said, the belief of so many in the 1950s, 60s and 70s that computers would always be a minority, industrial technology has clearly been proved plain wrong.

Today, a great many commentators seem to be of the opinion that very few people will ever want a 3D printer, and hence that the demand for them will remain very limited. As I have argued in this chapter, it is quite possible that only a minority of us will ever have a personal 3D printer at home purely because the most useful and sophisticated models will be shared online or in retail outlets. Even so, I would speculate that within 20 years, and perhaps in less than 10, most people in developed nations will regularly make use of a 3D printer to 'materialize' a digital design, or will be regularly purchasing products or spare parts that others materialize for them. It may also turn out that most people will have at least a little 3D printer at home, if only as a hobbyist tool or educational device. When a 3D printer can be purchased as a smartphone or tablet accessory for $99 or less (and this will happen well before the end of this decade), would you really never purchase one for yourself or your child?

Over the next decade or two, the 3D Printing Revolution has the potential to mirror the PC Revolution of the 1980s and 1990s. In fact, as I wandered around the 3D Printshow in October 2012, I was reminded of how it felt when I visited an early personal computing expo way back in 1987. At that time, PCs were only just starting to take hold and had touched very few people's lives. Even so, as I explored the 1987 PC expo it was very obvious that the foundations of a revolution were being laid. In a similar fashion, as I toured the 2012 3D Printshow it was clear that the metaphorical concrete required to support another radical technological transition was once again being poured. Granted, we do not currently have 3D printers that can easily manufacture most products in our homes. Nor does the hardware even exist for factories and retail outlets to offer widespread fabrication-on-demand. Yet it is increasingly obvious that within five to ten years, such technology is going to be possible.

Beyond the arguments presented in this chapter, there is increasingly strong practical evidence that the 3D Printing Revolution is revving up a gear. Not least, 2012 was undoubtedly the first year in which 3D printing started to capture mainstream media attention and the public's imagination. For example, in January 2012 the first real consumer 3D printer – the Cube from 3D Systems – was launched at the Consumer Electronics Show in Los Angeles. This offered out-of-the-box 3D printing to anybody with $1,199, and came with a USB key of 25 objects all ready for printout.

In addition to seeing the launch of the Cube, 2012 was also the first year in which people could purchase personalized, 3D printed chocolates (from ChocEdge.com), buy a 3D printer kit for under $400 (from Printrbot.com), and download a free app to turn a Microsoft Kinect games controller into a 3D scanner. In December 2012, Staples even announced the roll-out of a 3D printing service in its European stores in 2013. And as 2013 got underway, in his State of the Union address President Obama advocated the continued development of 3D printing as a technology with 'the potential to revolutionize how we make almost everything'.

All of the above were signature developments that may serve to bring the 3D Printing Revolution just one baby step closer. Yet for me, the most memorable 3D printing innovation of the last year or so was the launch of a $1,200 service called 'Form of Angels' from the Japanese pioneer Fasotec. Here an MRI scan is taken of a pregnant woman, and then used to produce a 3D printed model of her unborn baby. The plastic foetus can even be supplied embedded in a resin model of its mother's midriff for presentation on the expectant parent's mantelpiece.

As we head through 2013, 2014 and beyond, the speed and variety of the 3D Printing Revolution will continue to gather momentum. As it does so, there is also a danger that reality and fantasy will become blurred, and that really important developments will get lost in the hype. For all of those seeking a serious understanding of how 3D printing is likely to transform both manufacturing and our personal lives, some knowledge of what current and likely-future 3D printing methods can and cannot achieve is subsequently paramount. In our next chapter I will therefore detail every known 3D printing technology.

2

3D PRINTING TECHNOLOGIES

Many people already have strong opinions about 3D printing. On the one hand, some advocates get highly excited and believe that we will soon be able to fabricate almost anything in almost any location. Meanwhile, others are fearful of the potential impact of 3D printing on employment, or simply dismiss any pending '3D Printing Revolution' as no more than hype. Either way, in my experience, many of those with strong views about 3D printing often know very little about how the technology works and what its limitations are.

This chapter seeks to bring some clarity to the situation by providing an overview of all existing 3D printing technologies. While many such technologies exist, as we saw in the last chapter, most can be placed into one of three distinct categories. Firstly there are printers that form object layers by extruding a semi-liquid material from a computer-controlled print head nozzle. Secondly, there are printers that use 'photopolymerization' to selectively solidify a liquid with a laser beam or other light source. And finally, there are devices that 3D print by adhering particles of powder to achieve some form of 'granular materials binding'.

All three of the above broad categories of 3D printing technology can output final objects in a variety of different materials using a number of different techniques. Here I am going to detail all such 3D printing methods in turn, starting with the different variants of material extrusion, and progressing to explain all existing processes for photopolymerization and granular materials binding. By the end of this chapter you should therefore have a solid understanding of 3D printing technologies and related terminology. You should also know what kinds of things can and cannot be 3D printed using a specific method. This means that if you want to 3D print a spanner, a plastic casing, an aircraft component, an item of jewelry – or indeed anything else – then you will know which 3D printing technology is going to be most appropriate for your needs.

In this chapter I will feature the work of several pioneering research teams and will refer to a few particularly significant items of hardware. This said, with the focus here being on 3D printing technologies, I am not going to provide a lot of detail on specific 3D printer models or the companies who manufacture them. Such information is I assure you featured in several other chapters of this book. There is, however, more than enough detail and terminology to include in this chapter without chucking in a load of model numbers and brand names that change fairly regularly anyway.

THERMOPLASTIC EXTRUSION

Today the majority of 3D printers create objects by extruding a semi-liquid material from a computer-controlled print head nozzle. Although, as we shall soon see, this process can be used to 3D print objects in a wide range of materials – including metals, concrete, ceramics and chocolate – by far the most common material that is extruded is a melted thermoplastic.

The more you learn about 3D printing, the more you will discover that it is an industry in flux, with lots of different terms being thrown around that sometimes mean exactly the same thing. Not least this is the case when it comes to the labelling of the process that is used to build objects by extruding thermoplastics. Most obviously, the technology ought simply to be referred to as 'thermoplastic extrusion'. More generically, it is also well described by the label 'material extrusion', and indeed in June 2012 the global standards body ASTM International pronounced that the standard, generic name for this kind of 3D printing technology should be just that.

While the above may appear all well and good, things are complicated by the fact that thermoplastic extrusion was invented by a market-leading company called Stratasys that labelled it 'fused deposition modelling' (FDM). The term FDM is therefore widely used (and misused) to refer to thermoplastic extrusion, and even to material extrusion technologies more generally. Stratasys is, however, the only 3D printer manufacturer that can use the labels 'fused deposition modelling' and 'FDM', as it has them trademarked. Because of this, other companies refer to thermoplastic extrusion as 'plastic jet printing' (PJP), 'fused filament modelling' (FFM), 'fused filament fabrication' (FFF) or the 'fused deposition method'.

The above is, I grant you, a lexical nightmare! But it is also a situation that we just have to live with. To try and make things as straightforward as possible, throughout this book I will use the term 'material extrusion' to refer to all technologies where a semi-liquid material is extruded from a print head, and 'thermoplastic extrusion' to refer to all cases where the material involved is a thermoplastic. You should, nevertheless, keep in mind that many people refer to thermoplastic extrusion as 'fused deposition modelling' or 'FDM', even though this is a trademarked name used by just one 3D printer manufacturer.

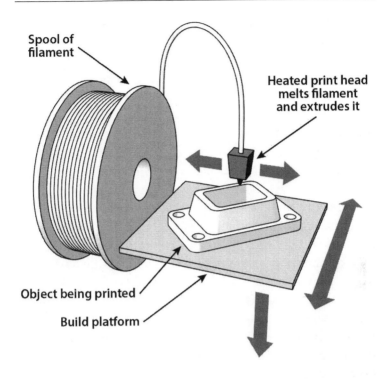

Figure 2.1: Thermoplastic Extrusion 3D Printing.

Moving on from the terminology jungle, Figure 2.1 provides an illustration of how thermoplastic extrusion works. Here a spool of build material referred to as 'filament' is slowly fed to a print head that is heated to between 200 and 250°C. This high temperature melts the filament, which is then extruded through a fine nozzle and flattened slightly by the print head on its way out.

Initially, molten filament is deposited directly onto a smooth, flat, horizontal surface known as a 3D printer's 'build platform'. Here the filament very rapidly cools and sticks, with the print head moving in 2D space to trace out the first layer of the object being printed. Some thermoplastic extrusion printers achieve this motion by moving the print head itself on both a North-South and a West-East axis. Alternatively, others slide the print head back-and-forth on one axis, while moving the build platform on another.

Once the first layer of an object has been traced out, the build platform lowers very slightly and the next layer of thermoplastic is deposited on top of it. This process then repeats and repeats – often over a period of many hours – until a complete plastic object has been printed. In essence, the whole process is a bit like building up an object with a computer-controlled hot glue gun.

While many materials can be used as thermoplastic filament, the most common is acrylonitrile butadiene styrene, otherwise known as 'ABS'. This is a type of thermoplastic that is widely used in industry to injection mold a great many products and parts thereof. For example, Lego bricks, cycle helmets and biros are all injection molded in various grades of ABS. In fact, if you are reading this book on an e-reader or other computing device, then its outer casing and buttons are almost certainly ABS injection moldings.

The fact that thermoplastic extrusion 3D printers can produce items in ABS – and hence with the same material properties as standard injection molded parts – really is very significant. Not least it means that manufacturers can 3D print things using thermoplastic extrusion and know exactly what they are getting without having to conduct extensive tests of their strength, durability, safety and other material properties. Where a small production run of up to about 5,000 ABS parts is required, it is also already sometimes cheaper to manufacture them with a thermoplastic extrusion 3D printer, rather than paying for molds to be made from which the parts can be injection molded in a traditional manner.

Spools of ABS filament are available as a 3D printing consumable in a variety of colours, with a typical filament being either 3 mm or 1.75 mm in diameter. Other common build materials used for thermoplastic extrusion include polycarbonate (PC) and ABS-polycarbonate composites. There is also a filament available called ABSi that can be sterilized with gamma radiation and ethylene oxide. This can allow plastic parts to be 3D printed for use in the food industry or for medical applications. ABSi also happens to be translucent, making it useful for producing items that need to transmit light, such as vehicle tail lamps.

Another material widely used for thermoplastic extrusion is polylactic acid, more commonly known as 'PLA'. This is a bioplastic that is currently made from agricultural produce such as corn starch or sugar cane, and which is subsequently far more environmentally friendly than ABS. PLA is also very safe to work with as it does not emit toxic fumes when heated, and is hence favoured by educators wishing to introduce children to 3D printers in schools or colleges.

PLA 3D printing filament comes in a variety of solid and translucent colours, and is popular with many 3D printing enthusiasts as it is even easier to print with than ABS. I will say more about future sources of PLA when we look at the environmental impact of 3D printing in chapter 6.

3D printers based on a thermoplastic extrusion printing process are already widely available, with an increasing number of models likely to enter the market over the next few years. Consumer thermoplastic extrusion printers can currently be purchased in kit form from around $400 upwards, or fully assembled from around $500. At the other end of the spectrum, the largest and most sophisticated industrial printers cost $10,000 or more.

Just as 2D printers have a maximum 'print area', so all 3D printers have a 'build size' or 'build volume' that determines the largest object they can print. For consumer thermoplastic extrusion printers, build volumes typically start at around 125 x 125 x 125 mm (or about 5 x 5 x 5 inches). At the time of writing, the largest build volume available on an industrial thermoplastic extrusion machine is 914 x 610 x 914 mm (36 x 24 x 36 inches). A build volume of this size can be used not just to make large objects, but also to manufacture many smaller objects side-by-side in a single print job.

THERMOPLASTIC EXTRUSION LIMITATIONS

Thermoplastic extrusion is a great 3D printing technology as it can produce small and medium-sized plastic items relatively simply in a tried and tested material. While this may all sound too good to be true, there are as always in life a few caveats to be aware of.

Firstly, in comparison to other 3D printing methods, objects created via thermoplastic extrusion may have significant stepping. In other words, when you look at a printed object up close it can be very obvious that it has been built up in layers. This may be particularly apparent on sloping or curved surfaces. Figure 2.2 provides a simple illustration of what a pyramid model produced via thermoplastic extrusion may look like in comparison to one made using traditional injection molding techniques.

Whether an object produced using thermoplastic extrusion will appear stepped or not depends on the resolution and accuracy of the 3D printer that created it. The best industrial printers can currently extrude plastic objects in layers that are 0.1 mm thin, and can also achieve an accuracy on their other two axes of about 0.1 mm. In comparison, printers that cost hundreds rather than thousands of dollars typically achieve a minimum layer thickness in the 0.2 to 0.5 mm range, and an accuracy on their other two axes of around 0.2 mm.

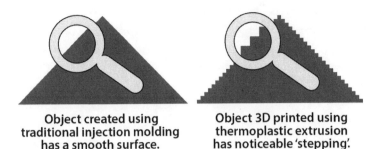

Object created using traditional injection molding has a smooth surface.

Object 3D printed using thermoplastic extrusion has noticeable 'stepping'.

Figure 2.2: Injection Molding v. Thermoplastic Extrusion.

It is generally accepted that the human eye cannot discern steps of less than 0.1 mm, although even when such a level of detail is achieved an object's surface is likely to feel somewhat rough. Indeed in practice today, no object produced via thermoplastic extrusion ever feels entirely smooth unless it has been lightly sanded after printout. This said, major 3D printer manufacturers do now claim that their latest 'production-quality' hardware is starting to rival the level of accuracy and surface quality achieved with traditional injection molding techniques.

Even when a thermoplastic extrusion 3D printer can produce objects in extremely thin layers, on occasion some users may choose to build things in slightly thicker layers in order to save time. After all, while an object that is 3D printed in 0.3 mm thick layers will be rougher than one printed in 0.15 mm layers, it will also take half the time to print. Given that some objects may take many, many hours to fabricate – I was recently shown a medium-sized product part that took 40 hours – such a time saving may be very significant. If the item being printed is a shelf bracket, door stop, lawnmower casing or a rough prototype, its surface quality may also be pretty irrelevant.

In addition to noticeable stepping, objects 3D printed using thermoplastic extrusion may warp, curl or shrink during printout, and sometimes significantly. This can occur as the material they are made from cools, with different parts of the object potentially cooling at different rates, in turn causing internal thermal stresses that tug things out of shape. To try and prevent this problem, most thermoplastic extrusion printers are fitted with a heated build platform. This stops the lower layers of their printouts from cooling significantly more quickly than those above them.

To further minimize warping or shrinkage, industrial thermoplastic extrusion printers feature enclosed build areas. These prevent drafts, and are carefully temperature controlled. Manufacturers of high-end printers – such as the FDM models from Stratasys – do now state that warping and shrinkage are no longer a significant issue.

The same claim can unfortunately not be made when it comes to most cheaper hardware. To try and deal with the issue, some low-cost thermoplastic extrusion printers have tiny fans fitted on the print head that point down to increase the cooling speed of the layers just printed. Many argue that warping and shrinkage can be reduced by printing objects more slowly, and by paying close attention to the starting height of the print head above the build platform. Another strategy is to print an object with a plastic lattice or 'raft' beneath its lowest layer. This has to be cut away or otherwise removed from the object after printout, but can help to adhere the object securely to the build platform, and hence to warp less.

Finally, regardless of printer type, warping may be controlled via effective object design. For example, reducing the level of 'infill' in an object may make it less likely to warp. While plastic parts created via traditional injection molding have to be entirely solid, items that are 3D printed may be

Figure 2.3: Overhangs and Orphan Parts.

hollow, solid, or made semi-solid by printing their insides as an open lattice. Making the inside of an object less solid will also usually reduce the chance of its innards pulling on and distorting its outside as it cools. Printing objects that are not entirely solid also takes less time and uses less filament, in turn reducing printing costs.

Another final and major issue to be dealt with is the support of any overhanging or orphan object parts during printout. To highlight the issues involved, figure 2.3 illustrates four plastic letters that we may consider creating on a thermoplastic extrusion 3D printer. Here, the capital 'L' can be printed with no problems at all. In contrast, the capital 'Y' has upward-sloping overhangs. This means that there is a risk of each successive object layer overhanging the one beneath it so significantly that it may fall away during printout. Here we would probably get away with the upper arms of the letter 'Y', as an upward slope that overhangs at no more than 45 degrees usually prints OK. But if we move on to the 'T', the upper parts of the letter jut out at a straight 90 degrees and would certainly fall away if no action were taken. Similarly, the capital 'M' may initially appear impossible to print, as during the early stages of the process the middle part of the letter would have to hang unsupported in space.

Of course, the 'T' and the 'M' could be printed quite easily just by outputting them lying flat on the build platform – and indeed optimal object orientation is critical when planning the 3D printout of almost anything. But unfortunately, many complex objects simply cannot be orientated so that they have no unsupported or initially orphan parts. To deal with this issue, almost all thermoplastic extrusion printers do on occasion have to print 'support structures' that keep everything in place. These temporary additions to the object then need to be removed after printout is complete.

Required support structures can be created in two distinct ways. Many cheaper thermoplastic extrusion 3D printers output a fine lattice of 'breakaway supports' using the same plastic material that they use to print the object itself. After printout, all of these extra bits of plastic must be removed with a knife or other implement, or else snapped-away by hand. Once the support structures have been removed, some further clean-up of the final object using sandpaper or other tools may then be necessary to remove any evidence that supports were attached.

More expensive thermoplastic extrusion printers create support structures using a second print head nozzle that outputs a soluble support material. Once an object has been printed, it is then placed in a tank containing a water-based detergent. An agitator in the tank circulates the solution around the printed object, with the detergent dissolving the support material away. A support-free 3D printed object is then removed, washed in clean water, and dried.

3D printers that output soluble supports inevitably involve their users in a messier and potentially more time consuming printing process than those that use breakaway supports. But they also deliver better results. Some 3D printer manufacturers refer to mechanisms that create and remove soluble support structures as 'SST' or 'soluble support technology'. 3D printers that rely on breakaway supports are then referred to as replying on 'BST' or 'break-away support technology'.

Although some level of support removal often has to take place, once this has occurred all objects produced via thermoplastic extrusion are ready for immediate use (although they may be sanded, coated or painted if required). In contrast, items produced using other 3D printing methods often require far more significant levels of 'post processing', such as curing or infusing with another material.

THERMOPLASTIC EXTRUSION IN PRACTICE

Thermoplastic extrusion is a mature and robust 3D printing technology that is relatively cheap, safe and mess free (and particularly so if objects are printed with either no supports or breakaway supports). Unlike many other 3D printing technologies, thermoplastic extrusion also creates objects in standard materials that are already widely used in industry and well understood.

While most thermoplastic extrusion 3D printers can currently only manufacture objects in one material (sometimes plus a support material), a few models are capable of outputting two or three different build materials at the same time. There are even experimental printers that can mix several different thermoplastics in their print head, so potentially allowing them to print plastic objects in full colour.

Thermoplastic extrusion 3D printers are already fairly widely used to produce concept models that allow designers to handle their creations and to show them to clients long before conventional manufacturing may take place. The technology is also used to produce functional prototypes of objects to allow the fit and movement of different components to be checked before conventional manufacturing commences.

A third use of thermoplastic extrusion 3D printers is in the creation of the patterns, molds, dies and jigs that are required to tool up a manufacturing facility in order to create objects via conventional means. Some forms of thermoplastic extrusion have even been created entirely for this purpose. For example, the so-termed 'drop on demand' (DOD) technology developed by a company called Solidscape (now owned by Stratasys) outputs objects in special wax-like plastics. 3D printers that utilize this technology are commonly used to produce sacrificial patterns or molds in dental labs.

While all of the above are significant, arguably the most revolutionary and growing application of thermoplastic extrusion is in the direct digital manufacture (DDM) of final products or parts thereof. As has been noted, where a run of a few hundred or even a few thousand thermoplastic parts is all that is required, their manufacture using a 3D printer can already prove more cost effective than turning to injection molding or other traditional techniques. Thermoplastic extrusion 3D printers costing $1,500 or less also already offer enthusiasts and small companies the only means possible to produce many kinds of plastic parts. I will say far more about direct digital manufacturing in chapters 5 and 6.

Today, thermoplastic extrusion is the most widespread form of 3D printing. In fact, some people seem unaware that any other form of 3D printing actually exists! Indeed, I have often been told that a 3D Printing Revolution is impossible because 'not everything in the world is made of plastic'. This latter statement is of course true. But it is also the case that material extrusion technologies – and indeed other 3D printing methods – can already manufacture objects in a wide variety of non-plastic materials.

FUSED DEPOSITION MODELLING OF METALS

Potentially a great many materials can be 3D printed using the process shown in figure 2.1. After all, many substances may be supplied to a print head in solid form, heated to become molten, and deposited under computer control. The only real issue is the complexity of achieving this with non-plastic materials.

A currently experimental if promising new variant of the technology is the 'fused deposition modelling of metals', otherwise known as 'FDMm'. Several instances have now been reported where standard thermoplastic extrusion printers have been modified to allow them to 3D print metal alloys. For example, a team led by Jorge Mireles from the University of Texas has conducted tests using a modified printer fed with a coil of metal alloy. The alloy used has to have a relatively low melting point (of less than 300 °C). But subject to this constraint, metals have been successfully heated and extruded to form objects in layers that were just under a millimetre thick.

Taking an alternative approach, other researchers have successfully adapted gas metal arc fusion welding robots to achieve the fused deposition modelling of metals. For example, researchers at Cranfield University have worked in partnership with Lockheed Martin to develop a form of FDMm that they call 'wire and arc additive manufacturing' (WAAM). The 3D printing hardware they have created is similar to a computer-controlled arc welder that also happens to extrude molten metal. As Mark Cooper reported for *Engadget* in November 2012, in a WAAM machine:

> . . . a thin wire of titanium . . . is threaded through a movable arm. Melted at the tip, it can then create objects of any shape as long as they are not bigger than the reach of the mechanism. While it's currently

a lot slower than traditional manufacturing, very little of the hugely expensive metal is wasted on the engineering room floor.

The team at Cranfield have successfully managed to 3D print many objects with their WAAM hardware. These have included a 180 mm high 'pint glass' that took about an hour to print and weighs about 3 kg. The WAAM hardware costs around £50,000, and can 3D print hollow objects in layers that are between 0.5 and 2 mm thick.

At present, while the fused deposition modelling of metals is experimental, in time it may become a mainstream industrial process for certain types of manufacturing. In theory, printers that can extrude both metals and plastics in the same build may also be developed.

MULTIPHASE JET SOLIDIFICATION

Another experimental form of extrusion-based 3D printing is multiphase jet solidification (MJS). Here, ceramic or metal powders are mixed with a 'binder' to create a filament strand (or sometimes a powder) that can be 3D printed using roughly the same process shown in figure 2.1. Many different materials may be used as a MJS binder, including a polypropylene thermoplastic or wax. The composition of the final filament or powder fed to the print head can vary significantly, but is typically about 60 per cent ceramic or metal powder and 40 per cent binder.

During the initial printing process the binder component of the build material is melted, and a high enough level of viscosity is achieved to successfully extrude it through a print head nozzle to form object layers. Once printout is complete, the resultant 'green' object then needs to have its binder removed. Depending on the materials used, this can be achieved chemically (by immersing the green object in appropriate solvents), or thermally (by heating the green object to a few hundred degrees centigrade so that its binder drains away). The resultant 'brown' or 'debound' object is then exceedingly fragile, and needs to be heated to a very high temperature. Depending on the materials being used, this final 'densification' stage typically takes many hours in a kiln heated to well over 1,000°C. Within the kiln, some shrinkage of the object usually occurs.

MJS was first tested in the mid 1990s, and at present has been superseded in commercial application by various forms of granular materials binding as I will discuss later in this chapter. Where MJS is used purely with ceramic powders, it is sometimes known as the fused deposition of ceramics (FDC). A British artist called Jonathan Keep has developed a DIY version of FDC that uses a 3D printer to extrude a semi-liquid clay with spectacular results. You can view examples of Jonathan's work and learn more about his 'potting in the digital age' at keep-art.co.uk.

THE MATERIAL EXTRUSION OF WOOD

Yet another experimental if proven material extrusion process allows for the fused deposition of wood. No really – it is now possible to 3D print wooden objects using a standard material extrusion 3D printer! To achieve this, a 3D printing enthusiast called Kai Parthy has created a 3 mm filament material called 'LAYWOO-3D'. This is a composite of wood fibres and a polymer binder, and can be melted and extruded to print wooden objects using any thermoplastic extrusion 3D printer, including consumer models that cost less than $1,000.

Once printed, objects created in LAYWOO-3D feel and smell like wood. They can also be sanded and otherwise worked on like any object made of a wood composite, such as medium density fibreboard (MDF).

One of the really clever things about LAYWOO-3D is that its final colour is dependent on the temperature of the print head used to melt and extrude it. In practice, this means that LAYWOO-3D can be output as either a dark or a light wood, or anywhere in-between. In fact, with appropriate temperature control, it is even possible to 3D print wooden objects with 'tree rings' or subtle colour gradients. If this were not enough, unlike thermoplastic build materials, LAYWOO-3D does not warp or shrink during printout.

THE MATERIAL EXTRUSION OF CONCRETE

While wood is one common material used to make buildings, another is concrete. Given that concrete is initially mixed into a viscous form that is poured before it sets, it is also not surprising that some researchers have begun experimenting with the material extrusion of concrete as a 3D printing process. Unlike the materials used in most other forms of material extrusion, concrete does not need to be heated to make it melt in a print head. Rather, it can be forced through a motion-controlled nozzle in its naturally pre-set state to form layers that then solidify.

The first experiments to create a 3D concrete printer took place at the University of Southern California in 2004. At the time the technique was called 'contour crafting', and was used to manufacture the world's first 3D printed wall.

More recently, the Freeform Construction Project at the University of Loughborough has created a 3D printer that uses a material extrusion process to output large concrete objects. The machine outputs a cement-based mortar from its print head, and has a build volume of 2 x 2.5 x 5 m (about 6.5 x 8.2 x 16.3 feet). While an earlier version of the printer was based on a 3-axis gantry, the most recent model has its nozzle mounted on a 7-axis robotic arm to further enhance print quality, speed and potential object size. Already the

Loughborough team have 3D printed a one tonne reinforced concrete architectural piece to demonstrate the viability of their technology.

One of the benefits of 3D concrete printing could be the fabrication of complex curves and designs that are hard if not impossible to manufacture with traditional building techniques. While at present all walls and floors cast in concrete have to be solid (as they are created by pouring concrete into some kind of mold or shuttering), 3D printing will relax this constraint. Parts of buildings will therefore be able to be crafted with internal air pockets to improve insulation and to reduce materials usage. Ducts for utilities like power and water will also be able to be 3D printed directly into a concrete wall as it is being made.

3D PRINTING CHOCOLATE & OTHER FOODS

One of the easiest to melt compounds that we encounter in everyday life is chocolate. The delicious substance is in fact the only solid that melts at human body temperature. The 3D printing of chocolate therefore ought to be relatively easy to achieve. And, as an already commercial technology, it actually is!

3D chocolate printing works pretty much like the material extrusion of thermoplastics, metal or wood. Chocolate is heated so that it melts, and is then extruded through a syringe-style print head under computer control. 3D chocolate printers have been created at several educational establishments, including the Massachusetts Institute of Technology (MIT) and the University of Exeter. The former have used their innovative hardware to 3D print people's faces in chocolate, while the latter have spun off a company – Choc Edge – that sells 3D chocolate printers for about £2,500. As a direct consequence, Christmas 2012 was the first with 3D printed customized edibles on the market, including chocolate Christmas trees, bells, snowflakes and snowmen with the recipient's name incorporated. To find out more, just visit chocedge.com.

Potentially several other foods may one day be commercially 3D printed via extrusion from a computer-controlled syringe. Many enthusiasts have indeed already successfully modified open source 3D printer designs to this effect. For example, in June 2012 an inventor called Sean Clanzer built a 3D printer that outputs icing sugar (frosting), and used it to decorate a cake. Meanwhile Marko Manriquez has created 'Burritob0t', a 3D printer that can extrude its user's desired combination of beans, rice, cheese, sour cream and salsa onto a warmed tortilla. To top it all, the whole process can be controlled via a smartphone app.

STEREOLITHOGRAPHY

As we have now seen, material extrusion is a form of 3D printing that can output quite a number of existing materials. It is also a technology that is relatively easy to construct, and which can hence be sold for a relatively low price. It is therefore unfortunate that extruding a molten or otherwise semi-solid material from a computer-controlled nozzle does have its limitations. Not least, it can take a very long time to make anything of a substantial size. Most objects are also prone to at least some degree of warping and shrinkage, and achieving a high-resolution printout can be problematic, especially across large build areas.

Due to the above, two other broad categories of 3D printing technology are in widespread commercial application. These produce objects in layers by either solidifying liquids or binding powders. The first of these methods goes under the general heading of 'photopolymerization'. This is based on the selective solidification of materials called 'photopolymers' which harden when exposed to an ultraviolet (UV) laser or similar controlled light source.

The first 3D printing technology to be invented was based on photopolymerization and is called 'stereolithography'. Stereolithographic 3D printers – otherwise known as Stereo-Lithographic Apparatus, or 'SLAs' – use a computer-controlled laser beam to build a 3D object within a tank (or vat) of liquid photopolymer. As in material extrusion, the object is created on a build platform, which in this instance is made of perforated metal and initially positioned just under the surface of the photopolymer in the tank. A UV laser beam then traces out the shape of the first object layer on the surface of the liquid. This causes it to 'cure' (set solid), and the build platform then lowers just a little. More liquid photopolymer then naturally flows over the top of the first object layer (or in some larger SLA 3D printers is forced across it by a mechanical mechanism that skims the surface of the tank), and the next object layer is traced out and set solid by the laser. This process then repeats over and over until the whole object has been printed. Finally the build platform is returned to the surface and the object is detached from it. Figure 2.4 provides an illustration of the stereolithographic 3D printing method.

As in material extrusion, objects 3D printed using stereolithography often require additional structures to be added to them to support overhangs or initially orphan parts. These supports then need to be broken away or otherwise removed with tools after printout. Once this has taken place, objects need to be cleaned with a solvent, and then a water rinse, to get a completely clean object. Often objects then need to be cured in a UV oven. Items created in transparent resins are sometimes also varnished to prevent discolouration if they are going to be exposed to sunlight. On occasion items may also have their surface quality improved by blasting them

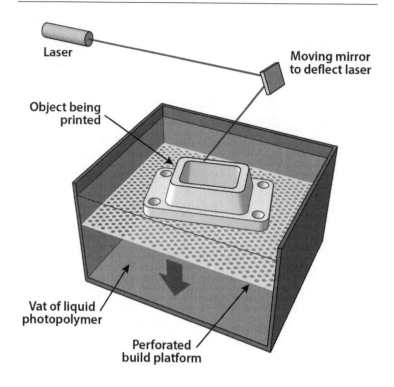

Figure 2.4: Stereolithographic 3D Printing.

with glass beads. Alternatively, they may be polished-up with a fine abrasive spray in a process known as 'vapour honing'.

Objects produced using stereolithography are very accurate and, unlike those created using material extrusion, have a smooth surface. The largest industrial stereolithographic printers can currently build models in layers that are only 0.05 mm thin, achieve an accuracy of about 0.025 mm on their X and Y axes, have a build volume up to about 1500 x 760 x 560 mm (59 x 30 x 22 inches), and can produce parts that weigh up to 150 kg. Such amazing printers do, however, cost between $100,000 and $500,000.

While stereolithography is a very high quality 3D printing technology in terms of resolution, surface quality, and the ability to print very complex geometries with a high level of repeatability, it has fairly obviously remained out of many user's price bracket. This is, however, just starting to change. For example, in November 2011 a company called Asiga launched a desktop stereolithographic printer for under $7,000. In May 2013 a $3,299 desktop stereolithographic printer called the Form 1 was then launched by Formlabs. Both of these devices solidify object layers on the bottom of a build platform that is then raised up out of a tank of photo-polymer liquid as each layer is created. The Form 1 has a build volume of 125 x 125 x 165 mm (4.9 x 4.9 x 6.5 inches), and can achieve a minimum layer thickness of just 0.025 mm.

When stereolithography was first invented it could only be used to 3D print objects in brittle resins. It was therefore typically used to produce masters from which final produc-tion molds would be taken, or else to make concept or display models. Today, however, a far wider variety of stereo-lithographic photopolymers have been developed. These include rubber-like plastics, many substitutes for ABS and other thermoplastics, flame retardant plastics, totally clear resins, and even special photopolymers for dental modelling and jewelry design. As a consequence, while stereolithogra-phy continues to be used to make mold masters and pre-production models, the technology is also starting to be used to manufacture final products or parts thereof. This said, the price of photopolymers does remain far higher than that of the build materials used in thermoplastic extrusion.

DLP PROJECTION

A second and equally impressive way to create 3D objects using photopolymerization is DLP projection. DLP (or 'digital light processing') technology may perhaps already be familiar to you, as it is increasingly found at the heart of many of the video projectors used in cinemas, lecture theatres, schools and some homes. DLP projectors feature a tiny imaging chip that contains an array of microscopic mirrors or 'digital micromirror devices' (DMDs). The mirrors can be rapidly rotated, so allowing them to reflect light out of the projector lens or onto a heat sink or 'light dump'. By controlling the orientation of the mirror array, a high quality image is created for projection.

So what, you may ask, have DLP projectors got to do with 3D printing? Well, the answer is that a DLP projector can be used to selectively solidify a photopolymer liquid. In a DLP projection 3D printer, a DLP projector is therefore positioned above a tank of liquid photopolymer, and is used to solidify an entire layer of an object on the surface of the liquid. As in stereolithography, the printer's build platform is then lowered, another layer is solidified by the DLP projector, and so on. Figure 2.5 illustrates the workings of a DLP projection 3D printer.

Like stereolithographic models, DLP projection 3D printers can achieve a high level of accuracy. Moreover, the accuracy obtained in smaller printers can be greater than that obtained in larger printers, as the projector image only needs to be focused on a smaller area. The largest current DLP projection 3D printers have a minimum layer thickness down to about 0.025 mm and a build volume of 267 x 165 x 203 mm (10.4 x 6.5 x 8 inches).

Already a great many photopolymers have been created for use as build materials in DLP projection 3D printers. These include opaque and transparent substitutes for traditional plastics, as well as wax-based polymers and several dental and medical-grade plastics. Indeed, DLP projection 3D printers from a company called EnvisionTEC are already fairly widely used to 3D print casings for hearing aids and in

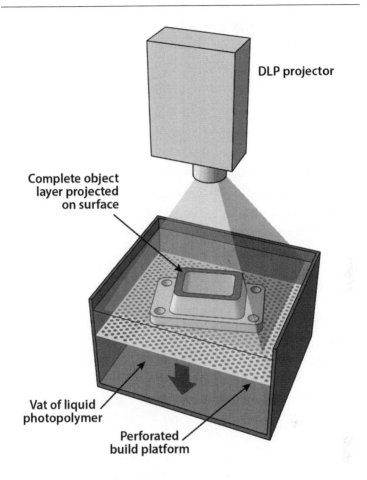

DLP projector

Complete object
layer projected
on surface

Vat of liquid
photopolymer

Perforated
build platform

Figure 2.5: DLP Projection 3D Printing.

the dental profession. I will say more about these applications in the next couple of chapters.

Because DLP projectors are fairly standard items, enthusiasts are already starting to use them to create their own DLP projection 3D printers. While more expensive to run than conventional thermoplastic extrusion enthusiast printers (due to the high price of liquid photopolymers), DLP very much has the edge when it comes to print quality. For a few thousand dollars, a competent amateur can now make their own DLP projection 3D printer that can print at a resolution of 0.1 mm or less, and sometimes using a DLP projector that can still be fairly easily removed to watch movies! I will explore this development in more detail when I look at open source 3D printing in chapter 5.

TWO-PHOTON POLYMERIZATION

A final 3D printing technology based on the selective solidification of a vat of liquid is two-photon polymerization (2PP). This is a 'nanophotonic' 3D printing method that is very similar to stereolithography, and which may well turn out to be a mainstream 3D printing process in the future. The technology is being developed by several research teams worldwide. These include Nanoscribe GmbH in Germany, and the Additive Manufacturing Technologies (AMT) group led by Jürgen Stampfl at the Technical University of Vienna.

2PP uses a 'femtosecond pulsed laser' to selectively solidify successive layers of a photopolymer resin. OK, so this probably sounds much like stereolithography. Well yes, until you learn that 2PP 3D printers have already achieved a layer thickness and an X-Y resolution of between 100 and 200 nanometres. So whereas conventional stereolithography has a resolution of about 0.025mm on its X and Y axes and a 0.05 mm layer thickness (Z axis), 2PP technology is achieving a resolution as tiny as 0.0001 mm on all axes.

To put it another way, 2PP 3D printing is currently about 250 times more accurate than conventional stereolithography, and capable of printing things far smaller than an average bacterium. 2PP is also far faster than stereolithography, and potentially capable of building up object layers at several *metres* per second! In the future 2PP may therefore enable the very precise 3D printing of very tiny things – such as microelectronic and optoelectronic circuits – as well as the rapid manufacture of larger objects.

To develop 2PP 3D printing, scientists in a number of disciplines in the Technical University of Vienna have worked to improve both photopolymer resin and mirror technologies. As reported by Don Fujiwara on 3DPrinterHub.com in March 2012:

> 2PP 3D printers work by putting down layers of liquid resin which are then hardened by a laser beam. A team of TU Vienna chemists led by Professor Robert Liska [have] developed specific molecules to embed within the resin. Called 'initiator' molecules, they react when struck by two photons (hence the name), which only happens at the exact center of the laser's beam. Once activated, the initiators trigger monomers throughout the resin to solidify.

> Mirrors were the second stumbling block to 2PP's need for speed. The process employs mirrors to guide the laser, and because those mirrors are constantly in motion, they have to be very precisely tuned to keep at pace. By figuring out how to move the mirrors faster and more precisely, our intrepid researchers were able to quicken print times by leaps and bounds.

To prove their metal, researchers in Vienna have already used their 2PP 3D printer to create a model of a Formula 1 racing car that is only 0.25 mm long, and which they printed in about four minutes. As illustrated in figure 2.6, they have

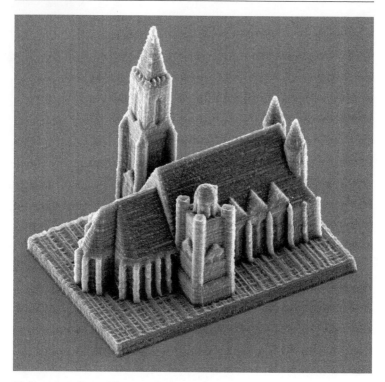

Figure 2.6: Two-Photon Polymerization.
This printout of St. Stephen's cathedral in Vienna was created by
Jürgen Stampfl's AMT group at the Technical University of Vienna
and is only 0.1 mm in length. Image reproduced with the permission
of Robert Liska.

also created an extremely tiny model of Vienna's St. Stephen's cathedral that is only 0.1 mm in length. Not to be
outdone, researchers at Nanoscribe have used their
Photonic Professional GT 2PP printer to create a detailed
3D print of a Hellcat spaceship from the Wing Commander
video game that is smaller in length than the width of a
human hair.

2PP 3D printing experiments have additionally involved printing scaffolds that may one day be used to help regenerate tissue in the human body by promoting natural tissue growth (a topic I will return to in chapter 7). While 2PP does remain a 3D printing technology in its infancy, its potential applications and implications really are quite staggering.

MATERIAL JETTING

Coming back down to earth, a final 3D printing technology based on the solidification of liquids is called 'material jetting'. Here a liquid photopolymer is emitted from a multi-nozzle, inkjet-style print head to form an object layer, and is then set solid with UV light before the next layer is added. While material jetting is the generic name allocated to this technology by the ASTM International global standards body, it is also known as 'polyjet' (short for 'photopolymer jetting'), 'PolyJet Matrix' (a term trademarked by Stratasys), 'multi jet modelling' (MJM), or 'inkjet photopolymer' depending on a printer's manufacturer.

Material jetting printers usually output support structures from their print head in a gel-like material that is removed after printout either directly by hand, or using a brush or water jet. Once all supports have been removed, no further post processing is then normally required. This makes material jetting technologies a lot less messy to implement than traditional stereolithography.

A very wide range of rigid, flexible, opaque and clear photopolymers have been created for use in photopolymer material jetting 3D printers. These include compounds that simulate the properties of ABS and other standard thermoplastics. Some printers also have the capability to output multiple materials in the same print job. Most notably, the Connex range of PolyJet Matrix printers from Stratasys can print in over 120 materials, and can output up to 14 of them in a single object. This is achieved by continually varying the mix of photopolymers supplied to a 96 nozzle print head. The largest printer in the Connex range has a build volume of 1,000 x 800 x 500 mm (39.3 x 31.4 x 19.6 inches). It can also print objects in layers as thin as 0.016 mm.

BINDER JETTING

As we head into the home straight of this overview of how 3D printing works, we come to our final, broad category of 'granular materials binding'. This refers to a very wide range of technologies that 3D print things by selectively sticking together the granules of successive layers of a very fine powder. Such powders can be made from many different materials – including plastics, metals and ceramics – and may be formed into solid objects in two distinct ways.

Firstly, there are printers that use a print head to spray a glue or 'binder' on to the build material. Secondly, there are printers that use some kind of laser or other heating technology to partially or completely fuse the granules of powder together. Here I will detail all current variants of both methods, starting with those that spray a binder onto powder.

Additive manufacturing devices that use an inkjet-style print head (and sometimes an actual photo printer inkjet print head) to spray a binder onto successive layers of powder are often the only hardware that purists and engineers refer to as '3D printers'. Unfortunately, this makes things kind of confusing for everybody else, as the technology concerned therefore often goes by the name of '3D printing' or '3DP'.

For specialists who refer to '3D printing' as 'additive manufacturing' this is all well and good, as using the '3D printing' label for the process that sprays a binder onto a powder clearly separates it from material extrusion, stereolithography and those many other technologies covered in this chapter. But for everybody else – and most people do now refer to 'additive manufacturing' as '3D printing' – it leaves things in yet another lexical mire. Back in June 2012, our old friends at the ASTM International standards body decreed that this kind of technology ought to be called 'binder jetting', and hence that is the label I will use here. This said, do please be aware that some people refer to this type of 3D printing by other names, such as 'inkjet powder printing'.

Whatever they are termed, binder jetting technologies are in widespread commercial use and can achieve excellent results. The build process starts when a layer of powder is laid on a build platform termed a 'powder bed'. This is usually achieved by raising the base of an adjacent powder reservoir and using a sweeper blade or a roller to push the powder so raised out across the bed. A multi-nozzle inkjet print head then travels across the powder bed, selectively jetting a binder solution onto it in the shape of the first object layer. The powder bed is then lowered, another layer of powder is laid down, another layer of binder is jetted onto it, and so on. Figure 2.7 illustrates the whole process diagrammatically.

When a complete object has been printed it has to be left to cure (for around an hour) in the 'cake' of dry powder within which it remains safely encased. Once curing is complete, some of the latest binder jetting 3D printers automatically remove most of the loose powder from around an object using a vacuum system that also recycles the unused powder for later use. At this point the object is then removed by hand from the powder bed and transferred to a 'depowdering chamber' in which it is sprayed with compressed air until it is completely clean. Depowdering chambers are built-in to the latest binder jetting 3D printers, and use a closed-loop negative-pressure vacuum system to recycle all

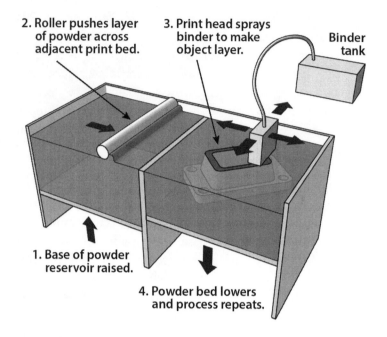

2. Roller pushes layer of powder across adjacent print bed.

3. Print head sprays binder to make object layer.

Binder tank

1. Base of powder reservoir raised.

4. Powder bed lowers and process repeats.

Figure 2.7: Binder Jetting 3D Printing.

excess powder so that practically no unused build material is ever wasted.

Many of the objects currently 3D printed using binder jetting technologies are output on 'ZPrinter' hardware that was initially developed by a company called Z Corporation, but which is now a part of 3D Systems. ZPrinters print in gypsum-based proprietary composite powders, such as 'zp150', 'zp140' and 'zp131'. Once objects have been printed in these materials they are quite brittle and very fragile. Hence, while they may on occasion be used as printed (for example as display models), most objects need to undergo some form of post processing. This is called 'infiltration', and involves brushing, spraying or otherwise coating an object with a chemical that will fill in microscopic air pockets and seal its surface.

Freshly printed or 'green' objects created on a ZPrinter can be infiltrated with a variety of chemicals. Objects that will receive minimal handling can simply be cured with a solution of salt and water. Those objects requiring more strength may alternatively be infiltrated with a one-part resin called 'Z-Bond', while objects that have to be really strong require infiltration with a two-part, high-strength resin called 'Z-Max'. Objects finished with the latter become very strong indeed, and may be used as functional prototypes and even final production parts. Items such as spanners and robot assemblies have, for example, been successfully manufactured using binder jetting with a Z-Max infiltration. Once suitably infiltrated, objects produced on binder jetting 3D printers can be sanded, drilled, painted and electroplated as required.

Binder jetting 3D printing is typically used to make prototypes, concept models and sometimes works of art. While the range of materials available is limited, the technology does have several major advantages over its material extrusion and photopolymerization rivals. Firstly, no support structures have to be printed or removed, as overhangs or orphan parts are always supported by the loose powder that surrounds an object as it is being printed. Secondly, the technology typically builds objects more quickly than alternative 3D printing methods. Thirdly, the price of objects created via binder jetting is typically lower than that achieved with other 3D printing technologies. And finally, binder jetting 3D printers are capable of outputting objects in full colour.

To make colour objects, binder jetting 3D printers spray coloured inks as well as a binder solution onto each powder layer as an object is being printed. The technology is exactly the same as that used in traditional, 2D photo printers, with cyan, magenta, yellow and black inks applied in an appropriate combination to produce full colour printouts. ZPrinter hardware is even clever enough to only spray ink a few millimetres deep into the surface of an object, hence saving on ink consumption.

The highest-specification ZPrinter currently on the market can print objects up to 508 x 381 x 229 mm (20 x 15 x 9 inches) and in 390,000 colours. The printer builds objects in layers of between 0.089 and 0.102 mm thin, achieves a feature accuracy on its X and Y axes of 0.1 mm, and can output up to 15 mm of material an hour. While these figures are impressive, to print very large objects a German company called Voxeljet has developed its VX range of 3D printers. These jet a binder onto successive layers of plastic powder or casting sand, with their largest model – the VX4000 – having a build volume of up to 4 x 2 x 1 m (about 13.1 x 6.5 x 3.3 feet). In part this is achieved using an extra wide print head that creates each layer in two passes.

3D SAND CASTING

Binder jetting 3D printers from Voxeljet and a few other manufacturers can be used to create molds or 'sand casts' that are then used to produce metal objects. For thousands of years, sand casting has been a common industrial process used to manufacture items in metals including iron, bronze, brass, aluminium and gold. The technique involves forming a mold by packing a special, resin-impregnated sand around a 'pattern' of the object to be manufactured. Such patterns are often made out of a material like wood that are relatively easy for craftspeople to shape.

Once the sand has been compacted around it, the pattern is somehow removed from the resultant mold in a process that may require the mold to be broken into pieces and reassembled. A molten metal is then poured into the mold to form into the shape of the pattern. Finally, once the metal has solidified, the sand mold is broken away to reveal the final object.

Dedicated sand casting 3D printers most often use a binder jetting 3D printing technology like that shown in figure 2.7. The material that is laid down in layers on the powder bed is a specially engineered sand, while the binder dispensed from the print head that moves over it is a foundry-grade resin. Once printing is complete, the loose sand that surrounds the object is removed, and the resultant mold is filled with metal in a normal sand casting process.

One of the key benefits of using 3D sand casting over traditional techniques is that there is no need to create a physical pattern of an object before it is printed (a process that today requires time and craft skills, or the use of another 3D printing technology). 3D sand casting also allows very complex and sometimes very large molds to be created that do not have to be broken apart to remove the pattern before casting. The use of 3D sand casting can therefore save a great deal of time and money, as well as allowing novel products to be created. While 3D printers that produce sand casts may not directly make 3D printed objects – and few of us may ever see one – they are nevertheless a very significant technology that will continue to greatly speed up and reduce the cost of one of our oldest manufacturing processes.

BINDER JETTING METAL PRINTING

Binder jetting 3D printers were first created to 3D print high resolution display models and prototypes in a special composite polymer. But some enterprising organizations have pushed the boundary and now use binder jetting to manufacture objects in bronze or stainless steel. Here, as in figure 2.7, a layer of metal powder is laid down and an inkjet print head moves across it to jet on a binder solution that glues together the metal granules where required. A heating lamp then dries the layer, and a fresh layer of powder is rolled over it. More and more layers are then printed to build up the final object.

Once all layers have been output, the 'powder box' containing the very fragile and porous object is placed in a curing oven at about 175°C for 24 hours. This evaporates any moisture and hardens the binder. All unused, loose metal powder is then removed, revealing a still-delicate object that is about 60 per cent metal and 40 per cent air.

To make the object stronger, it needs to be infused with more metal. To achieve this, the object is arranged in a box with bronze powder and surrounded by aluminium oxide grit to support it. It is then placed in a kiln for another 24 hours at over 2,000°C. Within the kiln the loose bronze powder liquefies to infiltrate the object and turn it into something that is at least 99.9 per cent solid metal.

Once cooled, the final object is taken out of the kiln. Any supports or 'sprues' that had to be added to facilitate the bronze infiltration must then be removed by hand. Most objects created using binder jetting metal printing are also polished as part of their final post processing.

Binder jetting metal printing is, as you can see, a somewhat involved undertaking (though do please appreciate that many objects are usually printed, cured and infiltrated in a kiln at the same time). Even so, the technology currently offers the cheapest form of 3D metal printing, and produces very strong metal objects in either bronze, or stainless steel infused with bronze. Build volumes are currently constrained to 750 x 380 x 400 mm (29.5 x 15 x 15.8 inches) with a minimum layer thickness of about 0.28 mm.

Binder jetting metal printing can offer a range of attractive surface finishes, including gold plating. The technology is therefore popular with some artists, including those who make jewelry.

BINDER JETTING CERAMIC PRINTING

A binder jetting process has also been successfully developed to allow the 3D printing of ceramics. Here successive layers of powder – such as an alumina silica ceramic – are laid down and sprayed with a binder. Once all layers have been printed, the object is dried in an oven, after which excess powder is removed. The object is then fired in a kiln, pre-glazed, fired again, glazed, and fired for a final time. The result is a shiny, ceramic object that is highly heat resistant and food-safe.

While final objects are smooth, the resolution of this kind of 3D printing is limited to about 2 mm on all axes, and not least due to the detail lost during the glazing process. Nevertheless, for the production of vases, plates, cups, bowls, egg cups and other tableware, the process is ideal. Several online 3D printing bureau now offer a binder jetting ceramics printing service, making the process available to anybody who wants to create their own custom tableware.

BINDER JETTING GLASS PRINTING

As yet another variant of the technology, some binder jetting 3D printers can create glass objects. As with ceramic or metal binder jet printing, a powdered material – in this case soda lime glass – is laid down in layers and its particles are selectively glued together by spraying on a binder. The resultant object needs to be cured in an oven, before being de-powdered. As in binder jetting metal printing, the resultant fragile object finally needs to be placed in a box with additional glass powder and fired in a kiln at 750°C. While in the kiln, the object becomes infused with some of the additional powdered material, which fills in the spaces within it to create a truly solid object that can survive reasonable handling.

Objects produced using binder jetting glass printing can currently be made in either white or black glass, and are porous, brittle, and feel rough when touched. The technology can at present only produce relatively small objects (around 75 x 75 x 75 mm, or 3 x 3 x 3 inches), and is generally used for making sculptures and other decorative pieces.

SELECTIVE LASER SINTERING

As I said a few pages back, 3D printing based on granular materials binding can use one of two methods to stick tiny particles together. The first, as we have now seen, is to glue them together using binder jetting, and then often to post-process the resultant object to improve its strength. Meanwhile the second method uses the selective application of heat to bond adjacent powder granules in a process generically termed 'powder bed fusion'.

3D printing using powder bed fusion can be achieved in a variety of ways, with the most widespread process being 'selective laser sintering' (SLS). Here a layer of powder is rolled across a powder bed, following which a laser beam traces out the cross-section of the first object layer. The heat from the laser 'sinters' the powder granules that it touches, so causing them to at least partially melt and fuse with adjacent granules. An illustration of the process is provided in figure 2.8.

SLS can build objects using a wide variety of powdered materials. These include plastics (such as nylon), metals, ceramics, sand (for 3D sand casting) and wax. If you are wondering why you may want to use a 3D printer to create a wax object, the answer is that it can be used as a pattern in a traditional casting process as described above. A benefit of creating a wax object master or 'pattern' is that it does not need to be removed from the mold that is formed around it, as when heated it will simply melt away. Wax objects created and used

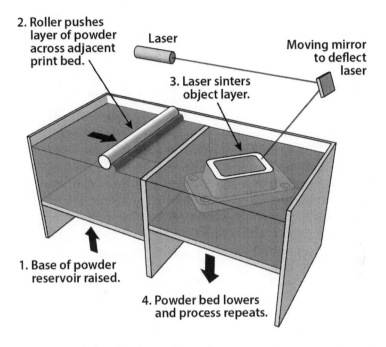

2. Roller pushes layer of powder across adjacent print bed.

Laser

Moving mirror to deflect laser

3. Laser sinters object layer.

1. Base of powder reservoir raised.

4. Powder bed lowers and process repeats.

Figure 2.8: Selective Laser Sintering.

in this fashion are referred to as 'sacrificial patterns' or 'sacrificial masters' as they can clearly only be used once.

Sometimes SLS 3D printers build objects from a two-component powder material. Here a powder with a high melting point (like glass or a metal) is mixed and in the process coated with a material with a lower melting point (such as nylon). This allows the laser to only have to melt the material with the lower melting point in order to fuse the powder granules into a solid. Recently a two-component SLS material called 'alumide' has become fairly popular. This is a plastic powder mixed with aluminium, and provides a means of fairly easily and cheaply producing objects with a metal sparkle at relatively low temperatures.

To make it easier for the laser to fuse powder granules together, an SLS 3D printer's build chamber is pre-heated to a temperature just below the melting point of its build material. SLS 3D printers that create objects in materials other than composite powders, plastics and waxes require lasers that can raise their build materials to very high temperatures. Because of this, so-termed 'pulsed lasers' are often used.

SLS is a very accurate process that produces excellent results when building objects in plastic materials such as nylon. However, the sintering (or non-complete melting) of two-part metal-and-plastic powders cannot produce final objects that have material properties suitable for some engineering applications, such as the production of engine components. Because of this, various special variants of SLS exist that use a laser beam to fully melt granules of a single-material powder – such as aluminium, steel, nickel alloys, cobalt chrome, iron or titanium – in order to produce far purer metal objects. All such processes have subtle differences depending on their implementation and the particular 3D printer manufacturer, and are variously known as direct metal laser sintering (DMLS), selective laser melting (SLM) and laserCUSING. The latter, for example, only differs from DMLS due to the fact that it uses more accurate lasers positioned closer to the powder bed, and with the hardware optimised to 3D print objects with a homogenous material structure. In contrast, most DMLS machines are optimised for printing speed.

DMLS, SLM and laserCUSING may all be referred to as 'additive metal manufacturing' (AMM) – a label that we could also reasonably apply to the fused deposition modelling of metals (FDMm) and wire and arc manufacturing (WAAM) technologies detailed earlier in this chapter. If you are getting fed up with the lexical quagmire of 3D printing technology then I can only sympathize that you are hardly alone!

Commercial SLS printers that 3D print in plastics, waxes and composite materials currently have a build volume up to about 550 x 550 x 750 mm (21.6 x 21.6 x 29.5 inches), and can achieve a minimum layer thickness of about 0.08 mm. DMLS and related technologies have a similar accuracy, if a smaller build volume (of typically 250 x 250 x 320 mm, or roughly 10 x 10 x 12.5 inches). This said, in October 2012 a German company called Concept Laser announced that it had worked with the Fraunhofer Institute of Laser Technology and funding from Daimler to create a very large 3D metal printer called the X Line 1000R. This has a build volume of 630 x 400 x 500 mm (24.8 x 15.7 x 19.7 inches), and can print in layers as thin as 0.02 mm.

The surface quality of final SLS/DMLS objects is excellent, and a range of finishes can be achieved. For metal objects, these include polishing up to mirror quality.

SLS and its metal-powered variants have an increasing range of direct digital manufacturing (DDM) applications. For example, as we shall see in chapters 4 and 6, the SLS of nylon has now been adopted for the customized manufacture of several different plastic products, while DMLS has found application in the production of aircraft components and other final engineering parts. One particular benefit of DMLS in aerospace is that it can be used to create sturdy but lightweight metal components by including open spaces or lattice work in areas of an object that would have to be solid if cast or otherwise manufactured via traditional means.

DIRECTED ENERGY DEPOSITION

Yet another means of creating final-use metal objects using a powder build material that is melted using a laser is 'directed energy deposition' (also known as 'laser powder forming'). Here a metal powder is directed into a high-power laser beam for deposition as a molten build material. Various companies have developed this technology, including Optomec, who refer to it by yet another (proprietary) name of 'laser engineered net shaping' (LENS).

A variety of materials can be printed using directed energy deposition, including stainless steel, copper, nickel, cobalt, aluminium and titanium. Unlike in SLS/DMLS and related powder-bed 3D printing processes, the metal powder fed to the print head can be altered continuously during printout. Directed energy deposition can therefore fabricate objects with properties that cannot be obtained using traditional production methods.

Directed energy deposition also has the advantage of being able to repair existing objects as well as fabricating new ones. While objects created using this technology do require some degree of surface finishing (such as machine polishing), they can otherwise be used directly after printout as fully-dense metal parts.

ELECTRON BEAM MELTING

Two final technologies that 3D print things using heat to selectively solidify powders do once again use a powder bed, but this time dispense with the laser. The first of these is electron beam melting (EBM) which, as you have probably guessed, uses an electron beam to achieve the process illustrated in figure 2.8.

EBM 3D printers have been pioneered by a company called Arcam, and achieve very high quality results by building metal objects layer-by-layer in a vacuum, with the electron beam making multiple passes of each object layer. The first of these passes scans the powder bed to pre-heat the build material to an optimal temperature. A second pass then melts the outline of the object layer, while the following passes melt the bulk of material inside the outline.

The technology involved in EBM is highly sophisticated, with the electron beam moved around via electromagnetic deflection, rather than a mechanical process. An advantage of EBM over DMLS and related technologies is that completely dense (or in other words 100 per cent solid) metal parts can be accurately created with zero distortion. In part this is due to the fact that they are 3D printed in a vacuum.

EBM's use is restricted to high-value build materials, such as various grades of titanium and cobalt chrome. Using these metals, final parts are now being manufactured using EBM for aerospace and other specialist industrial sectors. Medical implants have also been produced using the technology. Maximum build volumes for EBM are currently 200 x 200 x 350 mm (7.8 x 7.8 x 13.8 inches) on Arcam's A2 machine, with an accuracy down to 0.13 mm.

SELECTIVE HEAT SINTERING

Also pioneering a powder bed fusion 3D printing technology that is very similar to SLS is a company called Blueprinter. Their innovation has been to invent a process called 'selective heat sintering' (SHS) that uses a thermal print head to selectively solidify plastic powders. The key advantage here is the ability to create entirely solid plastic objects from powders with far lower-cost hardware than required for SLS, and also on the desktop.

Inside an SHS printer, a distributing blade spreads a powder layer across the powder bed. A thermal print head then scans across it to melt the required particles together. The process then repeats until a complete object has been printed and can be removed from the powder.

As with all powder-based technologies, SHS produces objects that do not require the addition of support structures, as the loose powder that surrounds the object during printout holds overhangs and initially orphan parts in place. In time,

SHS may therefore develop into a popular alternative to the 3D printing of plastics via thermoplastic extrusion. A desktop SHS Blueprinter currently costs about $13,000, has a build volume of 160 x 200 x 140 mm (6.3 x 7.9 x 5.5 inches), and produces models in powder layers that are 0.1mm thin.

LAMINATED OBJECT MANUFACTURE

As I said way back at the start of this chapter, almost all 3D printers work in one of three basic ways. As we have seen, these three broad methods are based on material extrusion, the solidification of a photopolymer liquid, or the bonding or fusion of powder granules. There is, however, a final and quite distinctly different approach to 3D printing that ought also to be on our radar. This goes by the name of 'sheet lamination', or more commonly 'laminated object manufacture' (LOM).

LOM builds objects in layers by sticking together laser-cut sheets of paper, plastic or metal foil. In the LOM process a feed mechanism advances a thin sheet of material onto the build platform. This material either has an adhesive backing, or at this stage has adhesive applied. A roller (sometimes heated) then passes over the sheet to press it into place. A laser finally cuts the outline of an object layer into the sheet, and the build platform lowers just a little. The process then repeats until all object layers have been created.

As with powder-based 3D printing technologies, objects created via LOM do not require support structures to be included, as the unused build material that surrounds them holds everything in place. To ease excess material removal, LOM 3D printers cross-hatch it with their laser during printout. This allows the unwanted paper, plastic or foil to be removed by hand in small blocks. Unfortunately, it then has to be scrapped, so making LOM the most wasteful 3D printing technology.

Back in 2001, one of the first 3D printers I ever saw in operation was an LOM machine about the size of a small automobile. The device was printing out a test design of the sole for a new pair of shoes, and making a very good job of it. In fact, by sticking together layer-after-layer of laser-cut paper laminate, the printer managed to create a very solid and quite beautiful sole that looked and felt like it was carved out of wood. (I should note that laser cutting can brown the edges of paper sheets very slightly). However, the quantity of waste laminate that ended up in the bin beside the machine was quite shocking, and I remember thinking that this had to be a transitory technology. Quite by chance, in 2012 I came across the very same machine gathering dust in a 3D printing research lab to which it had been kindly donated. Unfortunately, this particular LOM hardware only came with software drivers for Windows 3.1, and had therefore not been used in years.

LOM was invented by a company called Helisys in 1991 that has since gone out of business. Several other LOM 3D printer manufacturers have also entered and left the 3D printing marketplace since that time, and many commentators therefore dismiss LOM as a dead technology. This may, however, be premature, as recently some new LOM printers have come to market. These include a new plastic sheet printer from Solido3D, and a 3D printer from a company called Mcor that sticks together sheets of standard copier paper. The latter allows the 3D printout of objects at far lower cost than achievable with the other technologies outlined in this chapter. Mcor 3D printers have a build volume of 256 x 169 x 150 mm when fed with A4 paper, or 9.39 x 6.89 x 5.9 inches when fed with letter paper, and a resolution of 0.1 mm.

Mcor have even integrated a inkjet print head that can spray coloured inks onto each paper layer, so permitting the printout of full-colour objects that it describes as 'tough, durable and eco-friendly'. The Staples in-store 3D printing service mentioned in the last chapter is based on Matrix 300+ Mcor 3D printers. For the production of certain kinds of concept models and artworks, LOM may therefore still turn out to be a viable and popular 3D printing technology. It does after all 3D print in a readily available print material, and produces objects that require no post-processing.

A SOLID FOUNDATION

As we have seen, there are already many ways in which concept models, mold masters, prototypes and final product parts can be 3D printed in a range of materials including plastics, photocurable resins, metals, foodstuffs and ceramics. 3D printing may still be a revolution in its infancy. But there can be no doubt that it already has a very solid and wide-ranging technological foundation.

Since I wrote this chapter in early 2013, it is quite possible that new 3D printing technologies will have been invented. Some new 3D printing methods may even have entered common application. Not least this is because so many in-novative individuals are now recognising the potential for additive manufacturing. For example, Professor Lee Cronin from Glasgow University has plans to develop a 3D printer that he terms a 'chemputer'. This would allow people to 3D print pharmaceuticals at home. The build materials used in a chemputer would be simple chemical reagents that would react with each other on printout to form the complex mol-ecules from which pharmaceuticals are made. Already Pro-fessor Cronin and his team have begun work on a prototype chemputer, and hope to develop it to initially 3D print simple drugs like ibuprofen.

While we are on the subject of medicine, it is also worth noting that there is a whole other category of organic 3D printing technology that I have not included here. This is the fascinating if potentially frightening sphere of 'bioprinting', and will be covered in depth in chapter 7. Already bioprinting pioneers have managed to 3D print living human tissue, and one decade soon hope to be creating replacement body parts for transplant.

Returning to the present, this chapter has hopefully improved your understanding of current 3D printing technologies and their practical possibilities and limitations. With this knowledge now imparted, it is therefore high time for us to turn our attention to those companies who are driving the 3D Printing Revolution forward by manufacturing its hardware, writing its software, and offering 3D printing services.

3

THE 3D PRINTING INDUSTRY

All revolutions depend on the visions and labours of their pioneers. Over the past few decades, we have become rather spoilt by an 'Internet Revolution' that has proceeded at a rampant pace due to the ease by which almost anybody could create a website with the potential to become a dominant global brand. Most new online ventures may have failed. But because their main product has been information, many Internet pioneers have been able to get their business up and running with relatively little capital and minimal infrastructure investment.

When it comes to a revolution in physical manufacturing, the going is inevitably far more tough. As we shall see in chapter 4, many opportunities do now exist to use 3D printers to both improve existing manufacturing operations and to create entirely new businesses. Even so, somebody first has to invent and manufacture suitable 3D printing hardware, and such innovation is time consuming and costly. Granted, as I shall explore in chapter 5, a few 3D printing enthusiasts are now innovating low-cost 'open source' 3D printers. But their inventions only print in a narrow range of materials and are generally not suitable for industrial application. It may be heart-warming to ponder that the 3D Printing Revolution will be fundamentally driven forward by the part-time efforts of enthusiasts in their garages. Yet in practice this is unlikely to be the case.

In the last chapter I introduced you to a wide range of technologies that will be the basis of the 3D Printing Revolution. In this chapter, I am going to make your acquaintance with those pioneering organizations who actually invented these technologies, and who have subsequently invested and striven long and hard to bring them to commercial application.

Initially I will discuss those companies who actually make 3D printers. I will then turn my attention to 3D software pioneers, and finally to just a few of those organizations who offer revolutionary 3D printing services. Please note that my intention is not to detail every single company in these marketplaces, but rather to provide an industry overview that includes all major players, as well as some of the most innovative smaller pioneers.

3D PRINTER MANUFACTURERS

To many people's surprise, at the time of writing (in early 2013), no mainstream consumer electronics or computing company manufactures 3D printers. Rather, the 3D Printing Revolution continues to be driven forward by an entirely new wave of organizations who have always specialized in 3D printer production. Over the past few years, many of these innovators have merged to leave two companies – 3D Systems and Stratasys – as the dominant suppliers of 3D printing hardware. Each of these organizations is highly successful and growing rapidly. The shares of both 3D Systems and Stratasys are also publicly traded, with each company having a market capitalization of over $3.5 billion. The obvious place to start in any review of the 3D printing industry is therefore with an overview of 3D Systems and Stratasys.

3D SYSTEMS

In 1984 an inventor called Charles Hull was experimenting with specialist ultraviolet (UV) lamps that could be used to solidify liquid photopolymer resins. The intention was to improve the process of using a UV light source to set or 'cure' photopolymers used as a surface coating or in other traditional applications. However, Hull soon realized that the potential existed to solidify only certain parts of a tank of liquid photopolymer, hence allowing a 3D object to be created.

After many long nights and weekends, Hull developed an apparatus that could computer-control a UV laser beam. He then used this to trace and out and solidify a single layer of an object on the surface of a tank of liquid photopolymer. A perforated platform just below the surface of the liquid then lowered a fraction of a millimetre, so submerging this first layer just a little. The computer-controlled laser beam next traced out the second layer of the object, the platform lowered again, and so on. This process repeated until Hull had created a small, blue plastic cup.

With the successful completion of his groundbreaking experiment, Hull had invented 3D printing. After much development work, on 11th March 1986 he subsequently obtained US patent 4,575,330 for his 'Apparatus for Production of Three-Dimensional Objects by Stereolithography'. Also in 1986, Hull formed 3D Systems Corporation. Two years later, the company launched its first commercial 3D printer – or 'StereoLithography Apparatus' (SLA) – called the SLA-250. To make all this possible, around this time Hull and his team also created the *.STL file format that remains in use today as the most common language that allows computers to communicate with 3D printers.

Today 3D Systems is generally regarded as the world's leading 3D printing company, with reported sales in 2012 of

$353.6 million and a market capitalization in January 2013 of $3.75 billion. Since May 2011, shares in 3D Systems have been traded on the New York Stock Exchange (NYSE).

In addition to making stereolithographic hardware, 3D Systems also sells 3D printers that are based on thermoplastic extrusion (a process it terms plastic jet printing), selective laser sintering, direct metal laser sintering, material jetting, and binder jetting. Printers based on the latter technology (where gypsum-based powders are selectively adhered by spraying on a glue) were initially developed at the Massachusetts Institute of Technology (MIT) in 1993. The technology – which offers full-colour 3D printout – was in 1995 exclusively licensed to a company called Z Corporation that 3D Systems acquired in 2012.

3D Systems currently describes itself as 'a leading, global provider of 3D content-to-print solutions including personal, professional and production 3D printers, integrated print materials and on-demand custom parts services for professionals and consumers alike'. The company also advertises a 'commitment to democratize access and accelerate adoption of affordable 3D printing', and to this end also provides 'creative content development, 3D CAD software, curation services and content downloads'.

To achieve its envious market position, 3D Systems has in recent years gone on a purchasing spree and has acquired not just Z Corporation, but over 20 other 3D printing pioneers. These have included the 3D printing service provider Quickparts.com, 3D printed prosthetics pioneer Bespoke Innovations, the 3D printing design company Freedom of Creation, imaging specialist Vidar Systems, the 3D content supplier The3Dstudio.com, 3D software developers Alibre, Geomagic, Rapidform and Sycode, and a UK manufacturer of low-priced 3D printers and 3D printer kits called Bits From Bytes.

Most of the firms that 3D Systems has acquired have continued to trade under their original brand name as a '3D Systems company'. In addition, 3D Systems operates a further online bureau service called 3Dproparts, a 3D printing dental solutions service at toptobottomdental.com, and in 2012 created an online 'place to express yourself in 3D' called Cubify. Hosted at Cubify.com, the latter was launched pretty much concurrently with a $1,199 consumer 3D printer called the Cube, and strongly signalled the intention of 3D Systems to provide products and services to 3D printing enthusiasts and prosumers as well as to high-end industrial clients.

To drive the point home, in January 2013 3D Systems launched four new consumer/prosumer 3D printers. These comprised an updated Cube that prints twice as quickly, plus three new 'Cube X' models – the CubeX, CubeX Duo and CubeX Trio – that can output 'professional grade' models in one, two or three thermoplastic materials simultaneously.

Via Cubify.com, designers can sell collections of customizable 3D objects that 3D Systems prints and ships on demand. For example, visitors to Cubify can build their own 'Bugdroid' by dragging hats and other accessories onto an Google-Android-style robot.

There can be no doubt that the corporate drive and practical success of 3D Systems in spanning the whole 3D printing industry is extremely impressive. Some commentators are critical of the growth-via-acquisition strategy that has seen 3D Systems swallow up so many of its smaller competitors. This said, large, successful companies in which investors can have confidence are probably needed to bring 3D printing into the mainstream. Shares in 3D Systems increased in value by 247 per cent in 2012, and while such growth may be difficult to maintain, the continued rise of 3D Systems does seem extremely likely.

STRATASYS

Alongside 3D Systems, the other very major corporate player in the 3D printing marketplace is Stratasys. The company is of a very similar scale to 3D Systems, with its shares worth $3.52 billion in January 2013, and reported sales in 2012 of $359 million (a 30 per cent increase on 2011). Also like 3D Systems, Stratasys is the child prodigy of the inventor of a mainstream 3D printing technology.

Whereas 3D Systems was founded on the back of stereo-lithography, Stratasys Inc. was born following the invention of a material extrusion process called fused deposition modelling (FDM). FDM was devised by Scott Crump in 1988 following his decision to try and make a toy frog for his daughter by building it up in layers using a hot glue gun. The same year Scott established Stratasys with his wife Lisa, and in 1989 patented his FDM process. By 1992 Stratasys was shipping its first commercial 3D printer – the '3D Modeler' – and in 1994 went public on the US NASDAQ stock exchange. For a time Stratasys even owned the trademark on the term '3D printer', although in 1999 it allowed the phrase to enter the public domain.

Like 3D Systems, Stratasys has grown in part via acquisition, with the company having taken over or merged with Solidscape in 2010, and most notably Israeli 3D printing pioneer Objet in 2012. With the completion of its merger with Objet in January 2013, Stratasys Inc. became Stratasys Limited. While this acquisition was very significant (the biggest so far in the 3D printing industry), Stratasys has not to date gone on a competitor purchasing spree like that still being pursued by 3D Systems.

In addition to trading under its own name, Stratasys sells 3D printers under its Mojo, Dimension, Fortus and uPrint brands. It also provides a digital manufacturing service under the banner RedEye On Demand.

Following its acquisitions of Solidscape and Objet, Stratasys sells 3D printers based not just on FDM technology, but two proprietary processes it refers to as 'drop on demand' (DOD) and 'PolyJet Matrix'. DOD was invented by Solidscape, and builds objects from a wax-like thermoplastic to create dental wax-ups and castings. PolyJet Matrix is a specific material jetting technology invented by Objet, can output 120 different materials, and uniquely at the time of writing can 3D print objects in up to 14 different materials at the same time. This is achieved by jetting a mix of different photopolymers from an inkjet-style print head, setting the layer solid with UV light, printing the next layer, and so on.

Unlike 3D Systems, Stratasys currently focuses its business solely on serving high-end, industrial clients, with its customers including Boeing, Intel and Ford. While the market for entry-level 3D printers that create plastic objects is now expanding rapidly, to date Stratasys has shown no intent to launch consumer/prosumer hardware, even though it is the inventor of thermoplastic extrusion technologies.

ARCAM

As already noted, 3D Systems and Stratasys dwarf all other current 3D printer manufacturers. There are, however, a few other more specialist companies that are large enough to be publicly traded. The first of these is the Swedish pioneer Arcam AB, which had a share capitalization in January 2013 of about $97 million. The company's shares are traded on the NASDAQ OMX stock exchange in Stockholm.

Like 3D Systems and Stratasys, Arcam was founded on the back of a unique 3D printing technology, which in this instance was electron beam melting (EBM). Here object layers are created by fusing together the particles of a fine metal powder in a vacuum. The involved process is inevitably expensive and only 3D prints in high-value materials such as titanium and cobalt chrome. EBM does, however, produce very accurate objects with a high degree of material purity.

Arcam's roots date back to development work initially undertaken in collaboration with the Chalmers University of Technology in Gothenburg. By 1993 a patent application was filed for the process of 'melting electrically conductive powder, layer by layer, with an electron beam, for the manufacturing of three-dimensional bodies'. Arcam AB was then founded in 1997, with its first production 3D printer – the EBM S12 – launched in 2002.

Arcam states that its vision is to 'revolutionize the art of manufacturing complex parts'. Already its EBM 3D printers are in use within the medical implant, aerospace and defence industries, with 60 printers installed globally. As a particular milestone, in 2006 the Adler Ortho Group – an Italian manufacturer of orthopaedic implants – launched a medically certified hip implant that is manufactured using Arcam's 3D printers.

EXONE

At the time of writing, the most recently floated manufacturer of 3D printers is ExOne. The company had the initial public offering of its shares on the US NASDAQ stock exchange in February 2013, and in the process raised $94.4 million. The ExOne Company was founded in 2005 as a spin-off of the Extrude Hone Corporation – a company with over 40 years experience in non-traditional machining processes.

ExOne specializes in the production of binder jetting printers that 3D print in bronze, stainless steel, sand or glass. Their technology emits a binder from a print head to selectively bond successive layers of powder. When sand is printed, the resultant '3D sand castings' are used as molds into which molten metals are poured to produce final industrial parts. Alternatively, when bronze, stainless steel or glass powders are selectively adhered with a binder, the printed output is cured and infused with additional molten powder in a kiln.

ExOne describes its business as one that enables its customers to 'go beyond mass production' with 'imminent materialization' that saves time, money and the need for inventory, as well as permitting 'virtually unlimited design complexity'. Like Arcam, ExOne is relatively small, with just 13 printers sold in 2012. This said, eight of these were sold in the last quarter, and its machines do bear a price tag of between $100,000 and $1.4 million. As explained in the last chapter, 3D sand casting in particular has a very significant potential to save time and money in many traditional manufacturing processes, meaning that ExOne could have an exceedingly bright future. The first thing I ever personally 3D printed also happens to have been created in a stainless steel and bronze alloy using ExOne hardware.

ORGANOVO

At the time of writing, Organovo is the fifth and final 3D printer manufacturer whose shares are publicly traded. The company produces a 3D printer called the Novogen MMX that 3D prints layers of living human cells, and is at the forefront of research into organic 'bioprinting'. I have included Organovo in this listing of 3D printing manufacturers for completeness. But its work – along with that of other bioprinting pioneers – is so distinct and significant that I have chosen to devote an entire chapter to it toward the end of this book.

ENVISIONTEC

Aside from the aforementioned public companies, several smaller pioneers have also established themselves as successful 3D printer manufacturers. For example, a German company called EnvisionTEC has become a leading provider of what it terms 'computer aided modelling devices' (CAMOD). EnvisionTEC was founded in 2002, and now has headquarters and manufacturing facilities in both Germany and the United States, plus a sales and service centre in the United Kingdom.

EnvisionTEC's 3D printers build objects from photo-polymer liquids using DLP projection technology. Envison-TEC refers to this as its 'Perfactory' – or 'personal factory' – system, as its 3D printers are intended for use by those not expert in computer aided design (CAD) or manufacturing processes. The company also markets larger DLP projection printers under its 'Ultra' brand, as well as a '3D-Bioplotter' for use in tissue engineering. The latter is a very interesting device indeed, and is detailed along with the work of Organovo and other bioprinting pioneers in chapter 7.

EnvisionTEC's Perfactory printers are used for both pro-totyping and final part production. Industries that have adopted EnvisionTEC printers are as diverse as aerospace, architecture, jewelry making and toy manufacture, with the company's clients including Cartier, Ford, Disney and Games Workshop. EnvisionTEC 3D hardware is also used by dental technicians in the creation of crowns, bridges and temporary teeth. Another significant area of application is the use of the company's 3D printers by hearing aid manu-facturers to produce ear molds, as well as final product casings.

EOS

Founded in 1989, EOS is another German manufacturer of industrial 3D printers. The company specialises in printers that build items from powders using selective laser sintering (SLS), with different models available that are dedicated to making things in metals, plastics or sand. As with some of the 3D printers produced by ExOne, the 3D printing of sand allows for the creation of molds into which molten metal can be poured to produce final production parts.

CONCEPT LASER

Yet another company that has successfully applied German engineering to the production of 3D printers is Concept Laser. In this instance the technology involved is a unique one called laserCUSING, which can very accurately create final production parts from metal powders.

SLM SOLUTIONS

A fourth German manufacturer of industrial 3D printers is SLM Solutions. As the name suggests, this company produces a range of hardware that builds objects from powders using selective laser melting (SLM). While the company introduced its SLM technology to the market in 2000, it has only been trading under its current name since 2010 following the break-up of the previous MTT Technologies Group of which it constituted one element.

VOXELJET

Concluding our overview of German 3D printer manufacturers, we come to Voxeljet. Once again this is a business that produces 3D printers based on a powder technology. But this time the technology concerned is binder jetting, and used in 3D printers that can create either plastic objects or once again 3D sand castings.

Voxeljet currently makes five 3D printer models. The largest of these – the VX4000 – has an incredible build volume of 4 x 2 x 1 m (about 13 x 6.5 x 3.3 feet), so allowing very large parts to be created. In addition to manufacturing 3D printers, Voxeljet offers a range of related services, including 3D modelling, mold design, and casting in a range of metals. In May 2011, 3D Systems signed an agreement with Voxeljet to distribute its products in the United States.

DELTA MICRO FACTORY CORPORATION

Moving from Europe to Asia, our next established 3D printer manufacturer is the Delta Micro Factory Corporation. Based in Beijing, the company produces a wide range of 3D printer models for the Chinese market, some of which are available in the West.

Under their PP3DP brand, the company sells a range of low-cost, desktop 3D printers called UP!. These use thermoplastic extrusion to build plastic objects, and allow out-of-the-box 3D printing for non-specialist users. The same printers are also imported to the United States for resale by a company called Afinia.

OPTOMEC

Returning to the United States, Optomec is a pioneering manufacturer of 3D printers based on directed energy deposition. This technology deposits a metal powder that is melted with a laser to produce fully-dense, end-use metal parts. Optomec terms its implementation of this kind of powder fusion technology 'laser engineered net shaping' (LENS), and has now installed systems across 15 countries for over 150 customers.

Optomec was established in 1997, with its first LENS 3D printer delivered in 1998. By 2003 the company was working with Boeing, Rolls-Royce, Siemens and the US military, and since that time has continued to grow rapidly and win numerous awards. One of the key characteristics of its LENS technology is that it can be used not just to manufacture new end-user parts, but also to repair worn or damaged items. For example, LENS hardware may be utilised to fuse metal back on to a worn or damaged turbine blade.

In addition to its LENS hardware, Optomec has launched its 'Aerosol Jet' printers. These deposit materials onto surfaces – including 3D surfaces – to create printed electronic components. For example, Aerosol Jet hardware can print working solar panels, circuit interconnects or aerials onto the surfaces of other objects, such as aeroplane wings. The potential for the development and integration of this technology with other 3D printing processes is clearly very significant, making Optomec very much a 3D printing pioneer to watch.

MAKERBOT INDUSTRIES

Another 3D printer manufacturer that is doing really great things is MakerBot Industries. At the totally opposite end of the market to Optomec, MakerBot produces a range of low-cost, desktop 3D printers – or 'Replicators' – that use thermoplastic extrusion to create plastic objects. The company claims around a 20 per cent share of 3D printers sold, with over 13,000 MakerBots now gracing the desks of engineers, designers, researchers and enthusiasts around the globe.

Unlike those companies detailed thus far, MakerBot is one of the first organizational offspring of the 3D Printing Age. The company was set up in January 2009 by Bre Pettis, Adam Mayer, and Zach 'Hoeken' Smith, three friends who had been working on the RepRap Project. As I will detail in chapter 5, this open source initiative has the goal of bringing self-replicating 3D printers to the masses by creating free printer designs that anybody can download and build. However, not everybody has the skills and patience to get a RepRap 3D printer to work. Realizing this, Pettis, Mayer and Smith quit their jobs to set up a company that would

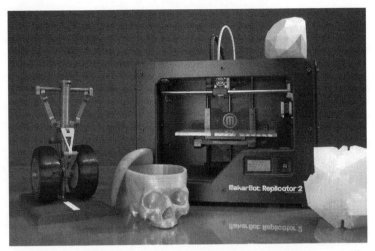

Figure 3.1: A MakerBot Replicator 2 with Printouts.
Image credit: MakerBot Industries.

start from the RepRap designs and create a low-cost, commercial 'robot that would make things', or 'MakerBot'.

MakerBot started out selling 3D printer kits for enthusiasts, with the first – the Cupcake – launched in 2009. Since that time, MakerBot has gone on to produce fully-assembled, highly professional 3D printers, including its iconic 'Thing-O-Matic' and most recently its 'Replicator 2'. The latter currently sells for a little over a couple of thousand dollars, and has been embraced not just by 3D printing enthusiasts, but also some big companies. You can see a MakerBot Replicator 2 and some of the things that it has 3D printed in figure 3.1.

A bit like 3D Systems, MakerBot has expanded its vision for 3D printing beyond the manufacture of hardware. Most notably, the company has set up an object-sharing community website called Thingiverse where MakerBot owners, and indeed anybody else, can access and contribute to a 'universe of things'. MakerBot was also the first 3D printer manufacturer to establish a retail store. This opened its doors at 298 Mulberry Street in the NoHo district of Manhattan in September 2012, and sells both MakerBot 3D printers and 'cool products' made using them. The idea behind the store was to leverage the fact that 'seeing is believing', with many people only really getting 3D printing when they can experience it happening in front of them in a physical space.

ASIGA

Another company that has been set up to bring 3D printing into a broader marketspace is Asiga, which launched its first model in November 2011. The approach the company has taken is to develop sub-$7,000 desktop stereolithographic 3D printers that use a UV LED light source to selectively harden a liquid photopolymer.

To produce a desktop device at its intended price point, Asiga has limited its hardware to a 'pico' build volume of just 40 x 30 x 75 mm (1.57 x 1.18 x 2.95 inches) on their smallest model. While this may appear somewhat limited, it is more than enough to allow the production of high-resolution dental pieces, hearing aid covers, jewelry designs, and associated patterns or molds.

FORMLABS

Taking a very similar approach to Asiga, another recent startup called FormLabs has also developed a low-cost desktop stereolithographic printer. Their Form 1 has a current retail price of $3,299, and a build volume of 125 x 125 x 165 mm (4.9 x 4.9 x 6.5 inches), making it a very significant competitor. Formlabs was spun off from the Media Lab at the Massachusetts Institute of Technology in 2011, and very clearly demonstrates the potential for a new generation of high-resolution 3D printers to be created at a previously undreamt of price point.

AND THERE'S MORE!

As we have now seen, the 3D printer marketplace is becoming quite well established, with companies from the United States to Europe and Asia producing a wide range of models based on a wide range of technologies. I could go on here to detail other pioneers – such as Mcor (who produce 3D printers that build colour models from layers of standard copier paper), or Printrbot (who build lovely, very-low-cost 3D printers with laser-cut plywood bodies). However, a very fair representation of the major commercial 3D printer manufacturers has been included above, and I will say more about the myriad of smaller firms trying to bring 3D printing into our homes in chapter 5. It is therefore now time to move on from companies that make 3D printer hardware to those who code 3D printer software.

3D PRINTING SOFTWARE PIONEERS

While all models of 3D printers can, in the right circumstances, do amazing things, like all computer hardware they are of no value whatsoever without appropriate software. We would indeed not be at the start of a 3D Printing Revolution were it not at least in part for the efforts of those who have coded the computer aided design (CAD) applications required to construct 3D models, as well as the control and post-processing software required to communicate digital designs with 3D printers.

The following sections contain a brief review of some of the key software houses that are contributing to the advancement of 3D printing. But before we get to them, it is worth remembering that the creation of 3D design software predates the invention of 3D printing. We should also note that a great many 3D computer modelling applications are used for traditional design purposes, as well as to create 3D computer graphics for use in print, television and movies. Because of all this, it should come as no surprise that few companies specialise entirely in 3D-printer-related applications.

It should also be noted that many of the 3D printer manufacturers listed above have developed software capable of taking industry-standard 3D design files and slicing them up into the *.STL or other file formats that can be understood by their hardware. 3D Systems has even recently launched an entry-level 3D printing design package called Cubify Invent. I have, however, not included any 3D printer manufacturers in the following sections, as software creation is not their primary business and they currently supply only minority products.

As in 3D printer hardware manufacture, two companies currently dominate the 3D printer software landscape. The first of these is Autodesk, and the second Dassault Systèmes. Both of these companies produce a range of CAD applications, with most commercially 3D printed objects likely to have begun their life in a version of either Autodesk's AutoCAD, or SolidWorks from Dassault Systèmes.

AUTODESK

Autodesk was established in 1982 by John Walker. Walker had obtained the rights to an early CAD program called Interact from its inventor Michael Riddle, and rapidly developed the product into AutoCAD. While Autodesk only started out with 14 part-time employees, it grew exceedingly rapidly and is now the largest design and animation software house in the world. By 1985, Autodesk had floated on the US stock market, and by January 2013 had a stock capitalization of $8.43 billion. The company now has more than 10 million users of its software, including the last 17 Academy Award winners for Best Visual Effects.

Autodesk is a highly innovative organization that sells a whole host of 3D design software. These include a high-end 3D modelling and animation package called 3D Studio Max, and versions of AutoCAD specifically for mechanical, civil or electrical engineering design. In December 2012, Autodesk established a partnership with bioprinting pioneer Organovo to develop software for the 3D design of replacement human tissues.

For those wishing to 3D print their designs, AutoCAD and other Autodesk products can directly export industry-standard *.STL files. Autodesk also works with a number of online 3D printing services to make obtaining 3D printouts from its software as easy as possible. This allows objects to be sent to a bureau for 3D printout from within the AutoCAD application.

In an acknowledgment of the widening demand for simple 3D modelling applications, in 2012 Autodesk launched a range of free consumer apps under the banner 'Autodesk 123D'. The include a basic 3D modelling program, as well as an app called '123D Catch' that can turn photographs into 3D models. Most recently, an iPad app called 'Creatures' was added to the mix. This allows 3D models of strange, new animals to be easily created. All Autodesk 123D apps can export *.STL files for 3D printout via a range of online services, and signal Autodesk's rising focus on the 3D printing marketplace.

DASSAULT SYSTÈMES

Dassault Systèmes is a French software house that describes itself as 'the 3D Experience Company'. In fact, the organization proclaims its mission is to provide businesses and people 'with 3D Experience universes to imagine sustainable innovations capable of harmonizing products, nature and life'. Like Autodesk, the company's 3D software products are used for a wide range of traditional industrial applications.

Dassault Systèmes was established in 1981 through the spin-off of a small software development team from Dassault Aviation. The company then grew rapidly and went public in 1996. By January 2013, the stock market capitalization of Dassault Systèmes was $13.63 billion, with the business boasting 150,000 customers around the globe. As you may have noticed, this makes Dassault Systèmes by far the largest company in the 3D printing industry in terms of stock market valuation (although like Autodesk and others, 3D printing comprises just one aspect of its activities).

For the creation of 3D printable objects, Dassault Systèmes most popular product is its SolidWorks CAD application. Like AutoCAD, SolidWorks can directly output *.STL files for 3D printout. It is also possible to control a 3D printer directly from within the program.

TRIMBLE NAVIGATION

While AutoCAD and SolidWorks are excellent applications, they are also complex and time-consuming to learn. The price tag for a full version of either package is also well over $3,000. Because of this, many non-designers and a rising tide of 3D printing enthusiasts tend to create objects in a number of other applications that are more accessible both technically and financially. While Autodesk's 123D apps do fall into this category, at present the most popular low-end 3D design software is SketchUp from Trimble Navigation. This is available in both professional and standard editions, with the former costing $495, and the later being free to download for personal use.

While SketchUp cannot natively create *.STL files for 3D printout, two plugins – CADspan and the i.materialise 3D printing plugin – may be easily downloaded to add this functionality. A wide range of free resources for those keen to learn SketchUp are also available online. For anybody who wants to start experimenting with 3D object design, SketchUp is therefore an excellent place to start.

The SketchUp software has had a somewhat interesting history. The program was first developed by a company called @Last Software co-founded by Brad Schell and Joe Esch in 1999. SketchUp then arrived on the market in 2000, to offer '3D for everybody' and immediately won awards for its ease of use. In March 2006, Google purchased @Last Software and made the standard version of SketchUp free for personal use. This inevitably expanded the product's user base, with over 500,000 downloads to date.

To many people's surprise, in April 2012 Google sold SketchUp to Trimble Navigation. While this initially alarmed the consumer 3D printing community, Trimble continues to allow the basic version of SketchUp to be downloaded for free. It is also continuing to partner with Google to run 'Trimble 3D Warehouse' – a free repository for sharing SketchUp objects online.

3D PRINTING SERVICES

Not all of those companies who have established themselves as 3D printing pioneers are the manufacturers of printers or the writers of computer code. Rather, a final category of those driving the 3D printing industry forward are providers of 3D printing services. Such organizations allow anybody to convert their digital designs into physical objects, and hence have an absolutely critical role to play in bringing 3D printing into the mainstream. Many commentators still believe that the 3D Printing Revolution will involve most people having a personal 3D printer in their own home. This said, I would personally hazard a strong guess that far more people will use 3D printing service bureaus than will ever own their own hardware.

Already there are literally hundreds of companies world-wide that offer 3D printing services, and the number is growing very rapidly indeed. The following therefore introduces you to just a few of the most popular and well known, and in particular to those whose services are accessible over the web.

SHAPEWAYS

Shapeways is a leading global 3D printing marketplace and online community. The company runs a website that allows anybody to upload a 3D design that can then be printed out and shipped back to them in a few days. In addition, Shapeways offers and integrates with a wide range of apps that allow those without design skills or specialist software to create their own 3D stuff. These include generic 3D printing CAD software, as well as dedicated apps that allow people to design their own custom cartoon characters, napkins rings, iPhone cases, vases and so on.

As well as offering a service to individuals, Shapeways allows designers to sell their creations from an online 'Shapeways shop'. All products sold from these virtual stores are printed-on-demand when somebody orders them, and currently include works or art, jewelry, homewares, miniatures and games. One design that has become particularly iconic is the 'Itty Bitty Sad Keanu Reaves' from a designer called 'neuralfirings'. This tiny figure is 3D printed in full colour and can be purchased in different heights that are equally sad.

Shapeways was founded in 2007 by Peter Weijmarshausen, Robert Schouwenburg and Marleen Vogelaar as a spin-off from Royal Philips Electronics in the Netherlands. It was developed under a scheme called the 'Philips Lifestyle

Incubator', and launched its 'print as a service' (PaaS) business in 2008. In 2011 the company relocated its headquarters to New York.

At the time of writing Shapeways can 3D print objects in over 30 materials that range from ABS plastics, alumide and ceramics, to photopolymer resins, stainless steel and sterling silver. The company has been termed the 'Amazon of 3D printing', and in March 2012 opened a 25,000 square foot factory in New York to potentially accommodate 30 to 50 industrial 3D printers. At least some of these printers could make up to 1,000 objects a day, giving the factory an estimated maximum production capacity of three to five million objects a year.

Unlike some 3D printing pioneers, Shapeways is already building up a very significant volume of activity that justifies investment in a large factory. By the end of 2012 there were over 230,000 registered members of its global online community, with more than 8,000 designers having set up an online store. By June 2012, the company had 3D printed and shipped its one millionth item, and by the end of the year was receiving over 10,000 object uploads a week.

MATERIALISE

Another 3D printing service pioneer that hails from mainland Europe is Materialise. The company is headquartered in Leuven in Belgium, and was established by Wilfried Vancraen in 1990, initially as a joint venture with the University of Leuven. Since that time the company has become widely-recognised as a veritable powerhouse of 3D printing innovation.

Materialise works with industrial clients to produce prototypes and 3D printed final products, as well as developing 3D software for specialist medical and engineering applications. These activities are coordinated through several divisions, including Materialise Industrial Services and .MGX. The former helps companies to produce prototypes and small production runs, while .MGX uses 3D printers to manufacture high-end design products that it then sells from its online store.

For the general public and individual designers, Materialise also offers an online service called i.materialise. Like Shapeways, this allows anybody to upload their 3D designs and get them printed out. Objects can be output in a wide 'Periodic Table of Materials' that includes ABS plastics, alumide, bronze, ceramics, gold, photocurable resins, silver, stainless steel and titanium. In addition, once an object has been uploaded and successfully printed, its designer can offer it for sale either via the gallery on the i.materialise.com website, or via their own web pages. As with the service offered by Shapeways, this allows anybody to create a product and to sell it without having to invest in any tooling or stock, as all items are printed on demand and shipped by i.materialise. When something is sold and manufactured, the designer simply receives a percentage commission.

SCULPTEO

Like Shapeways and i.materialise, Sculpteo is a web service that allows anybody to upload 3D models and get them printed out in a wide variety of materials. In a similar fashion to its competitors, Sculpteo also allows individuals or professionals to open up a store and sell their objects to other people. Sculpteo describes itself as the '3D Printing Cloud Engine', is headquartered in France, but also has a US office in San Francisco. The company was established in 2009, and began offering its online 3D printing services in 2011.

In comparison to its larger competitors, Sculpteo has done much to make its 3D printing services as accessible as possible to those new to 3D printing. For example, its website accepts object uploads in a very wide range of file formats. This allows 3D objects created in mid-price 3D animation packages – such as LightWave and TrueSpace – to be directly uploaded for 3D printout. Sculpteo also provides a number of plug-ins that allow design software like SketchUp to directly integrate with its service. Also available are a number of custom apps that allow anybody to create simple, customized objects such as key rings, iPhone cases, or 3D pictures based on an uploaded image.

AND MANY, MANY MORE!

As I said a few pages back, there are already a great many companies that offer 3D printing services. Not least, many 3D printer manufacturers have entered this rapidly growing marketplace, with 3D Systems offering its own Quickparts, 3Dproparts and Cubify Cloud 3D Print services, while Stratasys runs Redeye On Demand. There are also already companies that specialise in certain types of 3D printing service. For example, Figulo.com offers online ceramic printing for those who want to 3D print vases, tiles, sculptures and tableware.

A great many more companies offer industrial 3D printing. Typical of these is Proto3000 in Montreal, who can produce prototypes, tooling and other objects using all major 3D printing technologies, as well as offering 3D scanning, design and product development services. Similar companies include LPE (Laser Prototypes Europe) in Belfast, 3T RPD located in Berkshire in the UK, 3BIGGG.com in Paris, 3D Creation Lab in Staffordshire in the UK, GROWit in California, Inition, which has offices in both London and Melbourne, and Industrial Plastic Fabrications Limited in Essex in the UK. I mention these companies purely to give a flavour of the market. You can find a listing of all the companies mentioned in this chapter in my 3D Printing Directory. This is included at the end of this book, as well as being available online via ExplainingTheFuture.com/3Dprinting.

AN INDUSTRY ON THE RISE

Every year a company called Wohlers Associates produces a report on the 3D printing industry. Wohlers Associates was founded by Terry Wohlers, who has spent more than 25 years analyzing and forecasting the world of 3D printing. His annual report on *Additive Manufacturing and 3D Printing* has therefore become a well established and highly reputable guide.

The headlines from the 2012 report were that the sale of 3D printing products and services will reach $3.7 billion globally by 2015 (up from about $1.8 billion in 2012), and will surpass $6.5 billion by 2019. The industry grew at 29.4 per cent in 2011. Another interesting statistic was that in 2011 the sale of consumer-grade 3D printers (classed as those costing less than $5,000) surpassed the sale of industrial grade machines. As all of this indicates, 3D printing is an industry on the rise, and one of the few in which double-digit growth can be expected for years and probably decades.

As we have seen in this chapter, a great many pioneering organizations are now creating the hardware, software and services that are allowing the 3D Printing Revolution to firmly take hold. Not least, as evidenced by the rise of Shapeways, i.materialise and Sculpteo, the dream of creating final, physical products that are fabricated on demand has already become a reality. Granted, these are still very early days. Though as we shall see in the next chapter, more and more companies are starting to 3D print final products ranging from jewelry to spectacles, and vehicle parts to toys. The age of digital fabrication has therefore well and truly begun.

4

DIGITAL

MANUFACTURING PIONEERS

There are three, parallel ways in which 3D printing will drive a manufacturing revolution. The first involves the application of 3D printers to help produce concept models, prototypes, molds and other production tools. The second and third drivers then more radically involve the use of 3D printers as commercial manufacturing devices, or to facilitate personal fabrication.

In previous chapters I have indicated how 3D printing will help to improve traditional manufacturing by facilitating processes such as 3D sand casting. In this chapter I am therefore going to move on to focus on the business application of 3D printers to produce finished goods. Our next chapter will then look at current and future developments in personal fabrication.

According to Wohlers Associates, over 20 per cent of 3D printed objects are already final products or parts thereof. By 2020, Wohlers even expects this figure to rise to 50 per cent. If this proves to be the case, then by early next decade 3D printing will have finally shed its humble 'rapid prototyping' beginnings and fully morphed into a widely used manufacturing technology. This is not to claim that by 2020 any traditional manufacturing method will have been replaced by 3D printing. But, in at least some instances, 3D printing will have started to become the preferred production method.

It is already not difficult to find examples of one-off items that have been manufactured using a 3D printer. For instance, in 2011 engineers at the University of Southampton made the headlines when they managed to 3D print a flyable unmanned aircraft. Aside from its electrical and electronic systems, every part of 'SULSA' – the Southampton University Laser Sintered Aircraft – was laser sintered in nylon using an EOS 3D printer. All parts of the 6.5 foot wingspan vehicle were also designed to snap together so that no fasteners or glue were required. The plane even achieved a top speed of about 100 miles per hour. A similar unmanned aerial system (UAS) has been almost entirely 3D printed by Select-Tech Geospatial in the United States.

Moving to manned transportation, 3D printing has already been used to help produce a working, full-size car. The vehicle in question is an 'Urbee' – a revolutionary, low-energy, two-passenger hybrid vehicle created by Jim Kor of Kor EcoLogic, and claimed to be the first 3D printed drivable vehicle. In a strict sense this is not really true, as the engine, electronics and chassis were not 3D printed. Even so, Stratasys 3D printers were used to produce the vehicle's body in ten thermoplastic sections. While the first Urbee was an experimental creation, a second generation 'Urbee 2' already has 14 orders. This said, the vehicle has yet to go into commercial production, and not least because the body sections for each car would currently take about 2,500 hours to 3D print.

While at present neither the SULSA or the Urbee are mainstream products, a few 3D printed goods are now available for general purchase. In this chapter I am therefore going to tell you about those pioneering companies and individuals who are already using 3D printers to produce final products, components or works of art, or who have very credible plans to start doing so in the near future. Please note that this does not mean that the businesses mentioned are pressing 'print', raising a 3D printer hood an hour later, and lifting out a final item for instant dispatch to a customer. As we saw in chapter 2, virtually all 3D objects currently require support removal, polishing or other post-processing after they have been printed. Many applications of direct digital manufacturing (DDM) also result in components that need to be assembled into final products. Yet this does not negate the fact that there are already at least some products on sale that were 'materialized' using a 3D printer rather than traditional production methods.

3D PRINTED JEWELRY & ART

Many of today's 3D printers excel at the production of relatively small, high-value objects. Because of this, some of the first pioneers to delve into the world of digital manufacturing have been artists, and in particular those who make jewelry. Just one example of such a business is Nervous System, located in Somerville, Massachusetts. This was founded in 2007 by Jessica Rosenkrantz and Jesse Louis-Rosenberg, and describes itself as a 'generative design studio that works at the intersection of science, art, and technology'.

Nervous System has created a process that uses computer simulations to generate digital designs based on patterns found in nature. These are then 3D printed to create a unique range of rings, bracelets, earrings, pendants, lamps and other artworks that are sold from the studio's website at n-e-r-v-o-u-s.com. Prices start at $15 for a ring, and go up to $500 for a one-of-a-kind lamp with a LED fixture. Just four of the company's extensive range of 3D printed designs are illustrated in figure 4.1.

As the studio's manager, Aaron Holmes, explained to me, Nervous System's 3D printed products are fabricated by Shapeways. These include items produced in nylon using selective laser sintering (SLS), as well as designs output in stainless steel and bronze using binder jetting hardware from ExOne. Other pieces of jewelry are manufactured in precious metals like silver, gold or platinum by using a 3D printer to create a lost-wax object master around which a mold is created for sacrificial casting. To assist in its day-to-day design processes, Nervous System also uses an in-house MakerBot Replicator 3D printer.

Eager to learn more, I talked to Nervous System's co-founder Jessica Rosenkrantz to find out how the company got into 3D printing and why. As she recalled:

> We started making works using 3D printing in 2009 with our project Cell Cycle. We are interested in digital fabrication processes like 3D printing because they enable us to create complex, organic forms that would be difficult to create otherwise, and they allow us to create one-of-a-kind, customized products. Cell Cycle is a web-based app that allows people to design their own complex, cellular jewelry and sculpture that can be purchased and 3D printed.

Next I asked about the kinds of challenges that face digital manufacturing pioneers, and here cost was clearly a major issue:

> The main issues we've had to overcome have to do with price. Compared to other techniques for producing plastic parts, like injection molding, 3D printing is a very expensive process. We want to

Figure 4.1: Hyphae Brooch, Pendant, Rhizome Cuff and Ring by Nervous System. For more information or to purchase these items visit n-e-r-v-o-u-s.com.

make unique designs that [are] price competitive with traditionally manufactured goods. The service provider we work with – Shapeways – prices 3D prints by volume of material used to produce the item, so we've written software that creates designs with a small amount of material enclosing a large volume of space.

One of our collections, Cell Cycle, was inspired by the skeletons of radiolarians and is made up of cellular jewelry computed from a physics model of spring meshes. These cellular structures are very strong but have thin members. Our other 3D printed collection, Hyphae, is based on how veins form in leaves. After defining an initial surface and several starting points, or roots, we 'grow' a structure of veins on the surface. The result is a surface made up of very thin branches that interconnect into a closed cell network like the veins of a deciduous plant. With Hyphae, we are printing members that are at the limit of what Shapeways allows, but the overall structure's high degree of interconnectedness means they are still strong.

Finally I asked Jessica about her hopes and vision for 3D printing. Where did she see the technology heading? And what developments would she like to see? She replied as follows:

My hope for 3D printing is that the technology will continue to develop ways of allowing us to make better, more interesting products. Digital fabrication techniques like 3D printing are so exciting because they free us from the limitations of mass production. With no money invested in tooling and mold making, we're free to create more variation, and I think this will lead to significant diversification of products in the marketplace. Since the technology is much more accessible than traditional manufacturing, more people will be able to pursue their ideas and make products that meet their specific desires and needs.

3D printing also holds the promise of completely new types of materials. If you are using a computer to fuse together objects bit by bit, why use identical bits? Researchers are studying ways of 3D printing that involve dispensing different materials at once to create 3D prints that are amalgams of different plastics and metals. Functional components like conductive or resistive units could be printed to make electronic products straight out of the machine. There is also current research into printing modular materials (think very small Legos), so that objects made by printing could later be broken down into their initial materials. These are the developments I am watching most closely in the realm of 3D printing.

As our interview ended, Jessica assured me that as new 3D printing technologies emerge, Nervous System will be ready to explore them. And I have no doubt that this will be the case!

Another artist who has made a name for herself by utilizing 3D printing technology is Bathsheba Grossman. Like Nervous System, Bathsheba utilizes 3D printing bureau services (here i.materialise and Shapeways) to allow her to sell a range of metal and plastic sculptures and jewelry from her website at bathsheba.com. As with Nervous System, Bathsheba makes use of a range of technologies. These include the binder jetting metal printing technology developed by ExOne.

One of Bathsheba's specialities is the creation of fascinating metal sculptures based on highly complex mathematical forms. Just one of these is the 'Zarf', as illustrated in figure 4.2. Like other artworks, this can be ordered in a range of sizes. As Bathsheba explains on her website:

I'm an artist exploring the region between art and mathematics. My work is about life in three dimensions: working with symmetry and balance, getting from the origin to infinity, and always finding beauty in geometry . . .

I have a grass-roots business model. I don't limit editions, I price as low as costs permit, and most of my selling is direct to [customers] by way of [my website]. My plan is to make these designs available, rather than restrict the supply. It's more like publishing than like gallery-based art marketing: we don't feel that a book has lost anything because many people have read it. In fact it becomes more valuable as it gains readership and currency. With the advent of 3D printing, this is the first moment in art history when sculpture can be, in this sense, published. I think it's the wave of the future.

Intrigued by her innovative approach, I contacted Bathsheba to find out what led her to start making 3D printed works of art. As she explained:

I got into it because I was – still am – very attracted to sculptural forms that are difficult to produce by traditional manufacturing means.

The root of all my problems is undercuts: that's any sort of overhang, through hole, reverse draft angle, or other feature that makes it impossible to remove an object from a mold, without breaking either the mold or the object itself. My designs are all undercuts all the time, and before 3D printing that made them very difficult to produce as economically viable sculpture. The early part of my artistic career was very unpromising.

In the late 1990's I had a portfolio of designs that were too unmoldable to make, and too geeky to sell in galleries. Cheap 3D printing and web marketing

Figure 4.2: 'The Zarf' by Bathsheba Grossman.
For more information or to purchase this item visit bathsheba.com.

appeared at that time and suddenly those particular problems were solved.

Overall, this is the greatest time to be a designer since lost-wax casting was invented, 6,000 years ago or whatever, and in the long run this is going to be bigger than that was. Can't wait to see what's next.

Picking up on this point, I asked Bathsheba about her vision for 3D printing developments. In reply she was hopeful that new technologies for 3D printing in metals, ceramics, cloth, paper and wood were on the horizon. In particular she saw great potential for the direct metal laser sintering (DMLS) of precious metals like silver or gold, where there is 'very clearly money lying on the ground'. Bathsheba also had a very clear view of how innovation was likely to occur:

> What I don't see is incremental improvements in surface finish, pricing, material variety of existing processes. ExOne has found its market but not changed its process. Stereolithography is not very different from what it was 15 years ago. This industry proceeds only by quantum leapfrogs, as new companies with new patents appear.

3D PRINTED DESIGNER GOODS

Moving beyond art and jewelry, pioneers in the broader fashion and design arena have always been keen to explore innovative ways of developing a new look. It is therefore hardly a surprise that some designers are enthusiastically embracing 3D printing as the Next Big Fashion Thing.

Arguably the most influential early advocate of 3D printed designer goods has been Janne Kyttanen. During his graduate studies, this Netherlands-based designer imagined a world in which 'data was the design product' and in which 3D printing allowed things to be digitally stored and distributed 'in the same way that images and music travel through the Internet'.

In pursuit of his vision, in 2000 Janne founded Freedom of Creation (FOC), the first company to specialize in the sale of designer goods produced using 3D printers. The 'FOC Collection' has since grown to include high-end (and high price tag) designer lamp shades, tables, space dividers, trays and jewelry. There are even bags (made from a 3D printed chain mail 'fabric'), and fashion accessories including designer mobile phone cases. Most of the company's products are 3D printed in some form of white plastic, with the majority being laser sintered.

In a 2010 interview on the Shapeways blog, Janne described FOC as 'a pioneering design company busy with a new industrial revolution'. As he went on to explain:

> When I saw the first 3D printer, I immediately saw every object around me in wireframe and realized where this whole thing was going to go. I got quite obsessed with it quite early on and skipped making products by other means. For me it was so clear that I didn't see any point making anything by hand anymore.

In 2011 Freedom of Creation was purchased by 3D Systems. While the FOC brand remains, most of its designer collection is now sold through its new owner's online store at Cubify.com.

Also highly worthy of a mention here – and also sold via Cubify – are Olaf Diegel's range of designer, 3D printed electric guitars. Inspired by the idea of the 'ultimate heavy metal instrument, as seen through nature', these include models like the Spider LP Bass. This has a black, open-lattice body that resembles a web inhabited by large spiders. Other instruments feature atom or honeycomb 'hive-like' designs.

Each of Olaf's guitars is 3D printed in plastic, has a $3,000-$4,000 price tag, and can be customized in conjunction with Olaf to individual customer specification. As illustrated in figure 4.3, I saw one of these amazing instruments at the 2012 3D Printshow. And even though I do not play the guitar, I have to admit that it was seriously cool.

Figure 4.3: A 3D Printed Electric Guitar by Olaf Deigel.
Photographed at the London 2012 3D Printshow.

3D PRINTED SUNGLASSES

Heading into a designer market with lower price tags, a company called Protos Eyewear has specialized in the creation and sale of 'consumer grade 3D printed sunglasses'. Established in 2011 and based in San Francisco, the company sells its glasses from a website at protoseyewear.com, where a wide variety of frames are on offer. All products are 3D printed using selective laser sintering, with a 'proprietary mixture' of powdered materials used to achieve a high quality of finish. As Protos advertises on its website, the 'intricate layering process [of 3D printing] results in bold and striking designs that are impossible to make through standard manufacturing methods. Protos eyewear is lightweight and durable, and the material provides a unique look and feel'.

To find out more I chatted with Marc Levinson, CEO of Protos, and Richart Ruddie, its chief technology officer (CTO). I started out by asking why they decided to make 3D printed products, and what the advantages were. As Marc explained:

> 3D printing is finally beginning to reach a point where both the price and quality of printed materials are comparable to current manufacturing methods. [The] process allows us a great deal of flexibility, instead of printing large quantities of one design we can create as many (or as few) variations of styles and sizes as we need. We have also developed software that allows us to custom fit a pair [of sunglasses] to a customer's specific facial measurements.

I next asked about the company's vision for 3D printing and its possible future impact on their business. As Richart enthusiastically replied:

> We are very excited about the potential behind using 3D printing as a manufacturing method. With the help of our specific team, skills and software, our company is able to move very quickly when developing new products. We are also able to integrate our customer's feedback immediately and give them more say in what they can purchase.

Both Marc and Richart were also keen to stress that as 'the next industrial revolution begins' there will be a transition from products being made overseas, to more local manufacturing back in the USA. This is a view shared by many 3D printing advocates and pioneers, and is a subject that I will return to when we look at 3D printing and 'localization' in chapter 6.

3D PRINTED TOYS

Two other companies who were keen to be interviewed for this chapter, and who are already using 3D printing to escape the boundaries of traditional manufacturing, are MakieLab in London and ThatsMyFace.com, based in Beaverton, Oregon. Each has recognised the potential to use 3D printing to manufacture unique toy products, with their current business intended to serve as a stepping stone to larger plans ahead.

Based in Shoreditch in London, MakieLab describes itself as a 'new kind of toys and games company' that produces 'future-smashing' toys that are 'customisable, 3D-printed, locally-made, and game-enabled'. The company's first products are poseable 10 inch action dolls called MAKIES that anybody can design using a highly interactive app on the makie.me website. Given the sheer number of permutations available, every product shipped by MakieLab is unique.

Customers designing their own MAKIE have a choice of gender, skin colour, head shape, eyes, eyebrows, nose, mouth, hair, outfit, and even the width of the smile and the shape of the hands. Figure 4.4 illustrates the MAKIE creator web tool in action.

MakieLab was founded by Alice Taylor and Jo Roach in 2011 to 'model toys then manufacture toys overnight'. All of the doll's bodies are 3D printed in nylon using EOS selective laser sintering technology. Shoes and accessories like spectacles, snowboards, binoculars and laser swords are also laser sintered, with pre-production fast prototypes made on MakerBot Replicators. Clothing, eyes and wigs are

Figure 4.4: The MAKIE Creator from MakieLab.
You can access this web tool at makie.me.

then manufactured from other materials via traditional methods.

Recently I caught up with Jo Roach to find out more about the 'world's first 3D printed toys'. I started by asking her why the new company had decided to launch 3D printed products. As she explained:

> We decided to make 3D printed products because the toy industry is ripe for disruption: customisable, personal toys are far more interesting than generic made-in-China toys. They encourage creativity in kids before they even get to the toy store, and for MakieLab they allow local production and fast iteration. Customers can ask for horn rimmed glasses

on Monday and we can have them in the store by
Friday.

As with the other digital manufacturing pioneers I interviewed, I also asked Jo how she saw MakieLab's business
developing. And as with other firms the vision was clear:

> We want to be the next Lego, making toys that cus-
> tomers design for themselves. All kinds of toys, not
> only dolls. Our toys will interact with a game space
> on mobiles, tablets and the internet and be smart.

Also keen to leverage 3D printing to develop a wide-ranging, digital manufacturing business are ThatsMyFace.com.
As I mentioned back in chapter 1, this innovative company
allows customers to upload a front and side photograph of
their head, and from this generates a full-colour 3D model.
Via the magic of 3D printing, the customer's head is then
reproduced in miniature and added to a standard 4, 6 or 12
inch action figure (for example Batgirl, Superman or Wonder
Woman), or put onto the body of a Lego mini-figure. Alternatively, a miniature head can be purchased on its own, or
the customer's face can be turned into a full-size plastic mask
or 3D photograph. As with MakieLab, a host of customization options are thrown in for good measure.

ThatsMyFace.com creates its products using the full
colour, binder jetting ZPrinters made by 3D Systems. The
way in which they only have to 3D print part of most
products (as the bodies they stick their customer's heads
onto are standard toys) is also a stroke of genius. I was of
course keen to learn more about their business, and asked
their Sales Director, John Keaton, how they came to start
using 3D printing as a manufacturing process. As he recalled:

It was the only method back in 2008 to create a fully colored object from a 3D model at an attractive price. Although there is still labor involved, there is no artistic step required during the manufacturing step once the 3D model is made (say as opposed to a sculptor) which helps retain the likeness of someone's face.

We looked at CNC but there didn't seem to be a way to create a colored object. Other manufacturing methods such as sculpting, molds and thermoforming were too expensive or could not maintain likeness.

Looking to the future of 3D printing in manufacturing, John was keen – as so many others are – for hardware that offers larger print volumes, quicker print times, less post-processing of prints, more material options, printing of multiple materials at once, and lower consumable prices. Like other pioneers, he also had a clear vision of how 3D printing is likely to develop more generally, with bureau services to play just as important a role as personal 3D printers in the home. As John explained:

I expect retail 3D printing to become somewhat similar to current photobook printing services, where consumers send over their 3D models to be printed by local or domestic third parties. 3D printers will most likely remain expensive with space/expertise requirements for some time, especially as material variety increases. Individuals or collectives might still want to own their printers for privacy reasons or to manufacture items illegal in certain jurisdictions, such as weapons or copyrighted models.

As material variety increases and costs go down, I believe we'll see the emergence of game-changer killer apps (which the industry has yet to create - except ThatsMyFace of course ;-)). Becoming competitive with traditional injection molding will take time though, but might be precipitated by consumers' expectations for goods to be customized or to exhibit complexity currently not feasible with injection molding.

Finally I asked John if there was anything else he would like to communicate about ThatsMyFace.com. The answer? 'We'd like every kid to have their own custom action figure one day'.

MakieLab and ThatsMyFace.com are both very impressive operations. Both are also companies who have managed to develop cool, new software to help them bring customized 3D printed products to market. These firms are not, however, the only pioneers trying to transform the toy market with 3D printing. As a final if less grandiose example, a self-described 'bot maker, guerrilla product developer [and] newbie modeler' who goes by the name of Kidmechano has created 'Modibots'. These are an ever-expanding range of highly poseable 3D-printed action figures with a snap-fit, ball joint construction. You can perhaps best think of Modibots as a form of transformer-style, character-building Lego.

Kidmechano sells over 400 ModiBot figures and accessories (like different arms and shields) via Shapeways (the web address is shapeways.com/shops/kidmechano). And whereas the more visually polished MAKIES are priced at £99, and ThatsMyFace.com figures cost the best part of $100 or more, Modibot figures can be purchased for $15, with many accessories below $10. It is also not difficult to imagine that in time the Modibot or even MAKIE principle will go open source, with parents and children to exchange and iterate their own designs, so removing traditional manufacturers from toy production entirely. I shall say a lot more about this kind of possibility in the next chapter.

3D PRINTED PROSTHETICS

Moving from toys to life's more brutal practicalities, many 3D printing pioneers are starting to manufacture medical items. For example, Bespoke Innovations (a recent addition to the 3D Systems clan) is using 3D printers to laser sinter custom casings for prosthetic limbs. Known technically as 'fairings', these specialist coverings surround the often quite thin rods that make up a prosthetic leg, and accurately recreate the body shape of the limb that has been lost.

Until this point in time, most medical devices have been produced on a one-size-fits-all basis, and prosthetic limbs and their coverings have been no different. What Bespoke Innovations have pioneered is an approach that starts with the end user to create a product for them, rather than taking a generic product and fitting it to a patient. 3D scanning technology is used to capture images of the patient's 'sound side' leg and of their existing prosthetic. The former is then superimposed on the latter in 3D, and a fairing is designed for the prosthetic that mirrors the flesh-and-bone limb. This is then 3D printed and fitted, so restoring the body symmetry of the amputee. Those with prosthetics on both sides can use a 'stand in' to help the designers at Bespoke Innovations to produce fairings that best approximate their original body shape.

Bespoke Innovations was founded in 2010 by industrial designer Scott Summit and orthopaedic surgeon Kenneth Trauner. Their intention was to use 3D printing not only to 'return lost contour' to amputees, but in addition to allow a level of 'personality and expression' to enter the design of a truly custom prosthetic. As the company explains on its website:

> To this end fairings can be enhanced with patterns, graphics, and materials – including leather, ballistic nylon fabric, chrome plating, and even tattoos. By creating a unique custom form that presents the individual, Bespoke Innovations hopes to change the way the world thinks of prostheses.

While Bespoke Innovations is doing amazing work, fortunately very few people will ever need to make use of its services. Other prosthesis are, however, far more common, with many people having false teeth, crowns and fillings fitted in their mouths. Operating in this market, several 3D printing manufacturers now provide dental services and hardware, including 3D Systems, Stratasys and EnvisionTEC.

Already 3D printing is a well established dental technology, with many dentists or their labs using 3D printers to help create models of their patient's teeth. The required 3D data is gathered either directly using an intraoral scanner (that takes about two minutes to scan an entire mouth), or by indirectly scanning a traditional physical impression.

Most commonly, dental 3D printouts are used as molds or to otherwise assist in the production of crowns or false teeth via traditional means. Alternatively they may be used to help plan and practice complex surgery. However, it is now possible for final dental prosthesis to be 3D printed. As Jenna Franklin, Marketing Coordinator for EnvisionTEC, explained to me back in 2011, 'EnvisionTEC [already] has an FDA-approved material that the labs can actually produce long term temporaries with. Yes, they can print you new teeth!' Such 'temporary' teeth produced on EnvisionTEC

Perfactory 3D printers have even been worn by some patients for up to five years. By the end of this decade, many industry professionals expect that final crowns will be routinely and very rapidly 3D printed by most dentists in minutes. This will remove the need for their highly specialist production in a remote dental lab, and could reduce the requirement for a patient to visit a dentist on multiple occasions to have a crown fitted.

3D printers are also already being used in the direct production of teeth-straightening prosthesis. For example, a company called ClearCorrect uses material jetting 3D printers from Stratasys in the manufacture of its transparent plastic aligners. A computer model is created of the current and desired location of a patient's teeth. These are then used to 3D print a range of transitionary former models from which a progression of aligners can be created using traditional techniques. Both the aligners and the 3D printed formers that they have been made from are then sent to the patient's dentist. Supplying a 3D printed former with each aligner is a great innovation that can assist a dentist with fitting, as well as facilitating the rapid production of aligner replacements.

For Clear Correct, one of the biggest advantages of moving to 3D printed manufacture has been the ability to scale its growing operation simply by investing in more printers. Another critical benefit has been the ability to offer 40 per cent lower lab fees than other providers of clear aligners – so benefiting patients, doctors and the company's bottom line.

3D printers are additionally already widely used to make the outer shells of hearing aids. The involved process was invented by Jan Tøpholm, Søren Westermann and Svend Vitting Andersen of Widex, who christened it 'CAMISHA', or 'Computer Aided Manufacturing for Individual Shells for Hearing Aids'.

Initially a mold is made of a patient's ear canal. This is then laser scanned to produce 3D data that is used to design and 3D print an individual hearing aid casing. The required electronics are then fitted inside this custom shell. Today around 95 percent of all custom-manufactured hearing aids have their shells 3D printed, most often using hardware produced by EnvisionTEC or Stratasys.

3D PRINTED INDUSTRIAL PARTS

As we have now seen, digital manufacturing is starting to be adopted by at least some artists and consumer product pioneers, as well as having taken a strong foothold in dentistry and hearing aid manufacture. Outside of such relatively niche areas, at the time of writing nobody appears to be using 3D printers to manufacture whole products or large proportions thereof. This said, there is clear evidence that 3D printed components are starting to infiltrate some otherwise traditionally manufactured goods.

For example, as reported by *Industry Week* in March 2012, 'numerous companies are turning to additive manufacturing to build not only prototypes but also [final] parts'. Just one example cited is C&A Tool, a contract industrial manufacturer based in Churubusco, Indiana. Here laser sintering is being used to produce diesel-fuel injectors and other final parts 'in quantities ranging from one to a few hundred'.

According to 3D printer manufacturer 3D Systems, a very wide range of companies are now producing at least some final product parts using their printers. For example, selective laser sintering hardware is being used to produce low-volume runs of metal or plastic components in industries as diverse as heavy equipment manufacture, consumer products, sporting goods, packaging and garden equipment.

Similar claims are made by other 3D printer manufacturers, with Stratasys providing a range of case studies. For example, a manufacturer of custom motorcycles called Mercury Customs now uses a Dimension FDM printer not just to prototype new parts (a process that saves the company between $5,000 and $8,000 a month), but also to produce some final components. These include a unique LED light bar fender – called the 'Prolite' – that would be impossible to create solely with injection molding.

Another Stratasys client, Kelly Manufacturing, makes a line of aviation instruments. These include a 'turn and bank indicator' called the M3500 that informs pilots of the rate of aircraft turn. A key part of the M3500 is the toroid housing that contains the coil used to power its gyro. In the past this housing was made from a urethane casting, though this was hard to manufacture to necessary tolerances. The lead time for obtaining 500 castings was also three to four weeks, with new tooling required for every design change. Today, however, the M3500 toroid housing is 3D printed, with 500 parts produced in a single run overnight on a Fortus FDM 3D machine. The need for tooling has of course been eliminated. So too has the need to hand sand each final part, as the 3D printing process delivers an improved surface quality as well as increased dimensional accuracy.

As a third example, a unit called the Trainer Development Flight (TDF) based at Sheppard Air Force Base in Texas is tasked with creating components – such as aerials – for military training purposes. Using Stratasys FDM hardware, a 'wide majority' of these are now 3D printed. As well as speeding production, this has delivered cost savings of over $3.8 million, with savings over a 10 to 15 year period expected to rise to $15 million.

As we saw in chapter 2, technologies now also exist that enable final-use metal parts to be 3D printed. Many aerospace manufacturers – including Airbus Industries and Rolls-Royce – have indicated their intention to develop and adopt

3D printing for low-run manufacturing, and to help produce lighter parts with a lower level of materials wastage. Such developments may reap significant environmental benefits as well as time and cost savings, and will be discussed in detail in chapter 6.

Aiming even higher, NASA is intending to use 3D printing to directly manufacture intricate metal parts for its forthcoming 'Space Launch System' heavy lift rocket. Engineers at Marshall Space Flight Centre are already experimenting with a Concept Laser 3D printer that uses its proprietary laserCUSING technology to produce fully-dense metal parts. These are intended to form part of the rocket's second stage J-2X engines. As elsewhere, the intention is to be able to produce final components more rapidly and at lower cost than with traditional production methods.

NASA has also been testing the potential application of 3D printers to manufacture spare parts on the international space station (ISS), as well as on future Mars and other deep space missions. Technologies trialled have included electron beam melting (EBM), again for creating fully-dense metal parts. Nipping down to a store for spare parts is obviously not an option when in orbit or on the way to another planet. Next generation 3D printing technology may therefore be one of those broader benefits to be reaped from the ongoing US space programme.

Even more far out are plans by a company called Deep Space Industries (DSI) to use 3D printers to help in its quest to mine the asteroids. According to DSI, it will rely on a 3D printer called the Microgravity Foundry to help manufacture metal parts from space-rock nickel deposits. According to Stephen Covey, co-founder of DSI and inventor of the process, the really cool thing about their 3D printer is that it will be able to 'take its own parts, grind them up, and recycle them into new parts'. Personally I would suggest that if a real Microgravity Foundry is ever set to work on an asteroid, the fact it can turn a broken metal part into a new one will be way down the list of DSI's amazing accomplishments.

3D PRINTED BUILDINGS

Back down on Earth, plans are also afoot to start constructing buildings with huge 3D printers. The idea is to build up habitable dwellings in successive layers of jetted concrete or glued sand. This large-scale form of additive manufacturing is also well off the drawing board.

Just one of the teams making headway in this area is based at the University of Loughborough in the United Kingdom. Here the Freeform Construction Project has created a 3D printer that outputs a cement-based mortar from a print head, and which has a build volume of 2 x 2.5 x 5 m (about 6.5 x 8.2 x 16.3 feet). Using this device, already a one tonne reinforced concrete architectural piece has been printed to demonstrate the viability of the technology.

An even more advanced and highly enthusiastic pioneer of 3D printing for building construction is Monolite UK. Here an Italian engineer called Enrico Dini has created a massive 3D printer – or 'robotic building system' – called the D-Shape that enables 'full-size sandstone buildings to be made without human intervention'. The involved technology is environmentally friendly, and jets a binder from a print head to selectively adhere particles of sand. The result of each massive print job is a very solid building component – or potentially even an entire dwelling – that is formed from a marble-like sand composite.

As D-Shape claim, what they have created is nothing less than a new building technology that will 'revolutionize the way architectural design is planned, and building constructions are executed'. In the future architects will simply press an 'enter' key to 'make buildings directly', rather than relying on 'intermediaries who can add interpretation and realization mistakes'. As they further explain:

> Today's construction technology lags behind the available computer design technology. The new 3D CAD software allows architects to conceive and design constructions easily, but existing building methods do not allow the full potential of the new design software to be achieved.
>
> The Industry needs to resolve this problem and we believe that D-Shape is the innovative solution . . . . [The technology] allows a level of precision and freedom of design unheard of in the past. The human limitations of master builders and bricklayers will no longer hamper architects' visions. D-Shape competes with the traditional construction industry which uses cement, reinforced concrete, bricks and stones.

Physically the D-Shape printer consists of a large aluminium framework that can 3D print any construction that can fit into its 6 x 6 m (17.1 x 17.1 foot) build area. Printout takes place in layers that are 5 to 10 mm thick, and final objects then need about 24 hours to fully harden. The D-Shape can be fairly easily disassembled and reassembled to facilitate transportation. Hoped-for applications include the printout of bus stops, bridge portions, arches, gazebos, temples and 'fantasy buildings'.

Recently Monolite have been involved with a project by Fosters and Partners to develop plans for a 3D printable Moon base. This work has been commissioned by the European Space Agency, and has been investigating the use of lunar soil – or 'regolith' – as a building material. This would save on the time and cost involved in transporting traditional building materials to the Moon.

Foster and Partner's plans are for a four-occupant lunar base to protect against 'meteorites, gamma radiation and high temperature fluctuations'. Firstly, a base for the structure would be unfolded from a tubular module delivered by a rocket. Next, an inflatable dome would be extended over the base. Finally, a D-Shape printer would be used to deposit thin-layer after thin-layer of bound regolith over the dome to create a very solid structure that would resemble a 'natural biological system'. Amazingly, simulated lunar soil has already been used to create a 1.5 tonne mock-up, while smaller-scale 3D printing tests have been conducted in a vacuum chamber to mirror lunar conditions. In these austere times it is fortunate indeed that the European Union has euros to spare for such critical projects.

OUR FUTURE 3D PRINTED WORLD

In one of my first interviews for this book, a long-standing industry insider informed me that the only people currently manufacturing products using 3D printers were the military, and that 'nobody would tell me about that'. While this individual was exceedingly helpful and right on many matters, as we have seen in this chapter he was clearly wrong when it comes to direct digital manufacturing. Granted, these are very, very early days, with nobody having 3D printed a habitable Moon base just yet. But from Nervous System to MakieLab, Protos Eyewear to ThatsMyFace.com, it is clear that digital manufacturing is already a reality. And where these early pioneers have bravely first put their feet, others will sooner or later dare to tread.

Hopefully reading this chapter has left you with a strong impression of what is being digitally manufactured right now, as well as what may be 3D printed in the future. Certainly interviewing those pioneers featured herein has helped me in my understanding of our future 3D printed world. Yet perhaps more than anything, what has really struck me has been the sheer passion and energy of those individuals who are driving forward the 3D Printing Revolution.

Unlike so many industries, the 3D printing movement is still very much an open club in which innovation and experimentation are championed, and in which knowledge is being freely exchanged both for the common good and for the pure joy of fresh invention. What is more, as we shall see in the next chapter, such an energy and spirit are a characteristic not just of a few industrial 3D printing pioneers, but of a rapidly emerging community of individual 'makers'.

5

PERSONAL FABRICATION

I have encountered many fascinating individuals in my forays into the world of 3D printing. Just one of them is Andy Ide, the founder of the website 3D Printing is the Future (3dfuture.com.au), and the proud owner of a Mendel Prusa open source 3D printer.

Andy and I live on different continents, but via the magic of the Internet have chatted about 3D printing on many occasions. When I started writing this book, I asked Andy the fundamental question 'why should we 3D print?', and his answer was as follows:

> 3D printing lowers the bar in the technical skills needed to create an object. Rather than needing to be competent in a large number of skills such as industrial design, machining, welding and using a lathe, 3D printing allows anyone to simply download a design and then click a button to tell their printer to print it. It takes maybe an hour to learn how to do this. This will lead to a huge increase in productivity for the average person. This is by far the most exciting thing about 3D printing for me.

What Andy highlights so well is the potential for 3D printing to facilitate widespread personal fabrication. Since the Industrial Revolution, the vast majority of our possessions have been produced in a remote factory using machinery too complex and too costly for most individuals to operate and own. But with the arrival of personal 3D printers, no longer will this have to remain the case. As Andy further commented 'knowing that I don't need to learn a trade to print a complex shape is very exciting'. And it is this excitement and opportunity that this chapter is fundamentally about.

AN OPEN SOURCE FUTURE?

When the seeds of the personal computing revolution were being sewn in the late 1970s and early 1980s, the involved technologies and ideas propagated in two very different locations. The first were the research and development departments of companies like IBM, while the second were the home workshops and early computer clubs frequented by pioneering hobbyists. Both corporate R&D and garage innovation also had a highly significant role to play in the PC's early beginnings. Not least IBM's activities gave the world a standardized hardware platform, while the first Apple computers were designed and assembled by Steve Wozniak, a member of the Homebrew Computer Club.

Like early PC hardware, today's 3D printers are the offspring of both corporate and homespun wombs. Most of the 3D printers in commercial application today may have been manufactured by those companies – including 3D Systems, Stratasys, EOS and ExOne – that I detailed in chapter 2. Nevertheless, there are also a considerable number of 'consumer grade' 3D printers owned and operated by private individuals and research teams, and which have far more humble roots. Many of these have even been self-assembled, with most based on 'open source' designs.

'Open source' refers to any initiative where the involved intellectual property is made freely available, and most usually via the Internet. Within online open source communities, product designs, computer code or broader ideas are shared and iterated for the common good. Today, the popular face of open source development is epitomized by two pioneering communities that use the web to create and distribute free software. One of these is responsible for the Open-Office software suite (in effect a free Microsoft Office clone), while the other has developed the Linux operating system and applications. Each of these communities creates computer software and related source code that is freely shared online, and which may be used by anybody under appropriate public licences. To provide an example of the scale of activity we are talking about, OpenOffice has now been downloaded over 300 million times.

In the world of 3D printing, two separate initiatives have laid the foundation for widespread, open source developments. Each of these creates and shares designs for 3D printers that anybody is free to personally build or even to commercially manufacture. These open source 3D printing initiatives are called the 'RepRap Project' and 'Fab@Home', and are an excellent place to start in any exploration of current and future personal fabrication.

REPRAP

The RepRap Project was started in 2005 by Adrian Bowyer from the University of Bath. RepRap stands for 'replicating rapid prototyper', with the project describing itself as developing 'humanity's first general-purpose self-replicating manufacturing machine'.

From the outset the idea behind RepRap was to create 3D printer designs that would be freely available. Or as Adrian told Andy Ide when interviewed on 3dfuture.com.au:

> When one has a machine that self-copies, logic compels one to make it open source. The alternative is that one will spend the rest of one's life in court trying to stop people doing with the machine the one thing it was most designed to do.

RepRap is based on thermoplastic extrusion technology, with a spool of thermoplastic filament fed to a heated computer-controlled nozzle that deposits it in layers. All early RepRaps, and indeed most RepRaps today, output a single thermoplastic that is also used to form breakaway supports where required. There are, however, some RepRap printers that have two nozzles, and which can hence print objects in two separate thermoplastics. Designs also exist for RepRaps with single 'colour blending nozzles' (also known as 'mixer extruders'). These can mix two or three different coloured thermoplastic filaments in the print head, so permitting multi-coloured objects to be 3D printed.

Given that RepRaps only 3D print in thermoplastics, it should come as no surprise that they cannot entirely self-replicate. Nevertheless, as the RepRap website at reprap.org explains:

> Since many parts of RepRap are made from plastic and RepRap prints those parts, RepRap self-replicates by making a kit of itself – a kit that anyone can assemble given time and materials. It also means that – if you've got a RepRap – you can print lots of useful stuff, and you can print another RepRap for a friend.

What the above means in practice is that a RepRap can 3D print all of the custom, thermoplastic parts needed to create a kit for building another RepRap. In addition to these parts

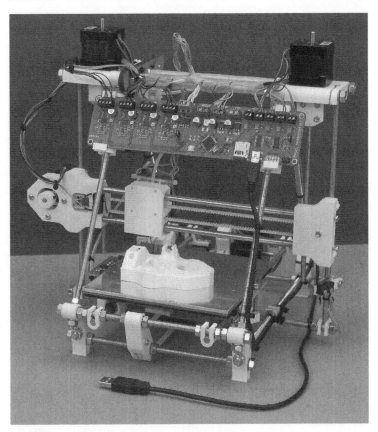

Figure 5.1: A Huxley RepRap 3D Printer.
Image: reprappro.com.

– which constitute about 50 per cent of the total device –
some fairly standard components are needed. These include
threaded rods, servo motors, wiring, electronic circuit
boards, a print head assembly (or 'hot end'), and a power
supply. Such parts can be obtained both individually and as
kits from a range of companies, including RepRapPro.com,
which is run by RepRap creator Adrian Bowyer. At the time

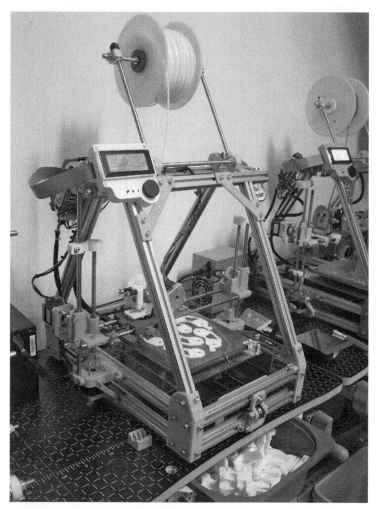

Figure 5.2: A MendleMax RepRap 3D Printer.
Image provided by RepRapUniverse.com.

of writing RepRapPro.com sells a full entry-level RepRap kit for $599 / £399, or a kit of everything aside from the 3D printed parts for $474 / £319. These prices include everything needed to get printing, though do exclude shipping. RepRap kits and spares can also be purchased from ReprapUniverse. com.

The initial RepRap design was called 'Darwin', and first constructed in 2007 (with its 3D printed parts made on a Stratasys FDM printer). In the Summer of 2009 an improved RepRap model called 'Mendel' was introduced and remains popular to this day. A standard Mendel is 500 x 400 x 360 mm in size (about 19.7 x 15.8 x 14.2 inches), and has an object build volume of 200 x 200 x 140 mm (7.9 x 7.9 x 5.5 inches). Other RepRaps now include the MendelMax (a design focused on structural rigidity and ease of assembly), the Prussa Mendel (a design focused on low cost and ease of component sourcing), the Wallace (which is a smaller 3D printer designed to reduce part count and to minimise build complexity), and most recently the Huxley (a currently experimental, travel-sized Mendel variant). A RapRap Huxley is illustrated in figure 5.1, while a MendleMax is shown in figure 5.2.

Because RepRap designs are open source, many pioneering individuals and some small companies have developed their own 3D printers using RepRap plans as a starting point. Most notably these include MakerBot Industries (as discussed in chapter 3, and which sells its MakerBot Replicators).

FAB@HOME

The second major open source 3D printing initiative is Fab@ Home. The first and foremost goal of this project is to 'facilitate the democratization of innovating by giving each household the ability to physically create their ideas'. Or as the project's website at fabathome.org further explains:

> Fab@Home will change the way we live. It is a platform of printers and programs which can produce

functional 3D objects. It is designed to fit on your desktop and within your budget. Fab@Home is supported by a global, open-source community of professionals and hobbyists, innovating tomorrow, today. Join us, and Make Anything.

The Fab@Home project was started in 2006 by Hod Lipson and Evan Malone in the Computational Synthesis Laboratory at Cornell University. The resultant Fab@Home community now includes hundreds of engineers, inventors, artists, students and hobbyists worldwide, and in its first year alone garnered over 17 million web page views.

Like RepRap hardware, Fab@Home 3D printers create object layers via material extrusion. However, unlike RepRaps and most other material extrusion 3D printers, Fab@Home hardware does not natively feature the controlled extrusion of a molten thermoplastic. Rather, Fab@Home printers use a syringe-based deposition system, with material forced out of one or more computer-controlled syringes by a piston. This allows a wide range of pastes, gels or slurries to be extruded. In fact, a Fab@Home can 3D print in any material that can be squeezed through a syringe and hold its shape, and which can then be hardened via drying, heating or exposure to UV light.

Already Fab@Home printers have created objects in a very wide range of materials. These include a specially-developed resin called 'FabEpoxy', silicone rubber, cake frosting, cheese, PlayDoh and gypsum plaster. Ceramic clay has also been successfully 3D printed after dilution with sufficient water, while chocolate has been output after fitting a small heater to the syringe print tool. Even hydrogel solutions containing living cells have been output by a Fab@Home (a subject that I will return to in chapter 7 when we look in depth at bioprinting).

The first Fab@Home 3D printer was called the 'Model 1', and was built at Cornell University in 2007. The design results in a printer that is 470 x 406 x 457 mm in size (or 18.4 x 16 x 18 inches), with an object build volume of 200 x 200 x 200 mm (or 7.9 x 7.9 x 7.9 inches). It takes between 18 and 24 hours to put a Model 1 Fab@Home printer together, with the parts costing around $2,300 for a single syringe device that can make objects in one build material.

Following the Model 1 into the Fab@Home stable was – as you may have anticipated – the Model 2. This is physically slightly smaller, faster, and more accurate, but features the same build volume. The Model 2 also costs less to build (at about $1,600), and can be fitted with interchangeable tool heads that can allow it (with hardware additions) to act as a computer-controlled milling device. The Model 2 can feature up to eight syringes for 3D printing in up to eight different materials. To ease construction, the Model 2 features plug-and-play electronics. To some people's surprise, the Model 2 was designed entirely by undergraduate members of the Cornell University Fab@Home student project team.

There is no doubt that the Fab@Home is an incredible in-novation. Yet as some of the above descriptions of it may suggest, it is more of a 3D printing research tool than its RepRap open source 'competitor'. Because it can create objects in a wide variety of multiple materials, the Fab@Home has already been used to 3D print some pretty amazing things. These include 3D printed cookies, working batteries, and even a functional telegraph machine.

OPEN SOURCE DLP PROJECTION 3D PRINTERS

RepRap has effectively cornered the 'market' when it comes to thermoplastic extrusion open source 3D printing. Similarly Fab@Home has done the same for the extrusion of other materials. Given that RepRap and Fab@Home designs are open source and can hence be freely amended and improved by anybody, we should also expect their 'dominance' to usefully continue. This does not mean, however, that opportunities do not exist to create open source designs for 3D printers based on other technologies. And this is indeed already starting to happen.

Most promising at present are open source designs for DLP projection 3D printers. As illustrated way back in figure 2.5, DLP projection is a vat photopolymerization technology that uses a DLP projector to selectively solidify object layers on the surface of a tank of liquid photopolymer. This may sound like highly complex stuff that would be difficult to put together in your garage or on a kitchen table. But today DLP projectors are standard audio visual equipment, and sometimes domestic equipment at that. Having purchased a DLP projector (and prices start at under $400), it is therefore becoming possible for a competent tinkerer to build a DLP projection 3D printer if they have access to an appropriate design. (Just in case you are wondering, the advantage of making this sort of open source 3D printer is that it will be able to create far more accurate printouts than possible with low-end material extrusion hardware such as RepRap or Fab@Home).

Several enthusiasts have now risen to the open source DLP projection 3D printer challenge. These include 'Lemon Curry', who has created designs for the imaginatively named 'Open Source Photopolymer DLP 3D Printer' and posted them at code.google.com/p/lemoncurry. As the website explains, the design 'already works in a lab with lab-grade equipment', with the intention being to create a final design and open hardware 'howto' that 'anyone with opposable thumbs and moderate thinking abilities might reproduce in the privacy of their own parent's basement'. Plans are also already being made for a second generation printer that will be able to solidify an object layer in under 0.2 seconds, hence allowing an object build rate of over 1 inch (25 mm) per minute. And that is very fast indeed!

A second open source DLP projection 3D printer is the Lunavast XG2. This has taken the clever approach of combining RepRap electronics with DLP projection technology to create an affordable but high resolution 3D printer. The project is in its early stages, but has already shown initial construction photos that look most impressive. The intention is to create an open source design that can be constructed for under $1,000, plus projector (or under $1,500 in total). You can find out more at reprap.org/wiki/Lunavast_XG2.

CONSUMER 3D PRINTERS

There is no doubt that open source 3D printers are cool. For DIY engineers, hardware enthusiasts and those who otherwise like to constantly innovate and tinker, they are also a great introduction to personal fabrication. Open source 3D printers can also deliver excellent results, providing that their operation is endowed with enough tender loving care and, dare I say it, a little luck.

The above important points made, and regardless of what many in the RepRap or Fab@Home communities may claim, open source 3D printers are not going to mainstream the 3D Printing Revolution. Rather, like very early built-in-a-wooden-box PCs, they will prove invaluable testbeds for technologies and ideas that companies will evolve into reliable, easy-to-use products for mass adoption. The development of MakerBot Replicators from early RepRap designs already stands testament to this cold economic reality.

What will turn personal fabrication into a mass market phenomenon are two things. The first will be the widespread availability of reasonably-priced 3D printing service bureau, while the second will be the emergence of low-cost personal

3D printers. I mentioned service bureaus like Shapeways and i.materialise in the last chapter, and will say a little more about them toward the end of this one. So for now let us turn our attention to low-cost 3D printers that can in theory allow non-technical individuals to start 3D printing things an hour or two after opening the box.

According to top industry analysts Wohlers Associates, consumer-grade 3D printers are those with a price tag of $5,000 or less. At the time of writing, this means that the highly successful $2,799 MakerBot Replicator 2X from MakerBot Industries is a consumer model. So too are the CubeX, CubeX Duo and CubeX Trio from 3D Systems at $2,662, $3,227 and $4,276 respectively. And, at $3,299, the amazing, stereolithographic Form 1 from FormLabs is also a consumer grade machine.

The aforementioned 3D printers are certainly and increasingly being purchased by companies large and small, as well as by a few private individuals. This said, to suggest that a consumer 3D printer is one that costs less that $5,000 is I think ridiculous. Not least in the ongoing climate of austerity that blankets all Western economies, few individuals are going to be able to fork out this much money for entirely personal use. I remember when 2D laser printers cost around $5,000 – and at this price point nobody ever considered them to be consumer tech.

To really go mass market, 3D printers will have to cost less than $500. The chances are, many models at this price or less are likely to arrive on the market in large numbers between 2015 and 2020. Even today, as we shall soon see, a few pre-assembled 3D printers can be purchased for about $500. But as they are few and far between, I shall herein define a 'consumer' 3D printer as a pre-assembled piece of personal fabrication hardware that costs around $1,500 or less (or about £1,000 or less in the UK). Granted this is still a lot of money for most people to have idly lying around to spend on a 3D printer. Nevertheless, I would argue that in the next couple of years it will be 3D printers in the $500 to $1,500 price bracket that will drive forward personal fabrication in the home, as well as in many schools and colleges.

Just before I discuss a few, real purchase options for those wishing to be brave pioneers(!), a couple of generic points really need to be firmly understood. Firstly, all pre-assembled 3D printers that cost less than $1,500 print objects using a single thermoplastic build material (ABS plastic or the bioplastic PLA), and have to output any required object supports in this material as well. This therefore has to limit the kinds of things that can be made. If you only want to make stuff in thermoplastics then one of the current crop of personal 3D printers may well be a great investment. But if producing items in metals, ceramics or other materials is more your thing, you will need to upload your designs to a 3D printing bureau.

Secondly, it must be appreciated that devices that cost $1,500 or less – and indeed devices that cost $5,000 or less – do not 3D print to anywhere near the level of quality of industrial hardware. Some proud personal 3D printer owners will tell you that this is not true. But sadly they are deluded. This is not to suggest that sub-$5,000 or sub-$1,500 printers are not amazing things with a very wide range of uses if you want to fabricate your own thermoplastic stuff. But, as we saw in the last chapter, pioneers like Nervous System and MakieLab use 3D printers in this price bracket for internal prototyping only, and not without good reason.

THE 3D SYSTEMS CUBE

The one major Western 3D printer manufacturer that sells a true 'consumer' model is 3D Systems with its entry-level 'Cube'. At a current sales price of $1,532 (until very recently it was $1,199), this just about fits into the 'consumer' price bracket I have chosen, and certainly allows out-of-the-box 3D printing for non-techies at home. The Cube is even equipped with a touch-screen interface and WiFi so that it can be used anywhere, and not necessarily close to a computer. When a Cube is not on a WiFi network, objects for printout may be supplied to it via USB key. Such a key is supplied with each Cube, and comes pre-loaded with 25 cool objects that you never knew you wanted, let alone wanted to 3D print. A Cube 3D printer is pictured in figure 5.3.

As the figure shows, and in contrast to all of its current competitors, the Cube actually looks like a consumer appliance. The printer is fed thermoplastic filament via a plug-in cartridge, with 16 colours available. These include the usual suspects you would find in a child's colouring box, plus glow-in-the-dark neon green and neon blue. All colours are available in either ABS or biodegradable PLA thermoplastics. The Cube's build volume is 140 x 140 x 140 mm (5.5 x 5.5 x 5.5 inches).

Many 3D printing enthusiasts are somewhat dismissive of the Cube. In part this is because it comes from a large, industrial 3D printer manufacturer, offers little opportunity to tinker, and is pretty much impossible to hack. This said, reviews suggest that it is solid and reliable. I have personally seen many Cubes in action, and have always been impressed with the quality of printouts given the price of the machine. Personally, if I were going to spend about $1,500 on a 3D printer I would buy either a Cube or an UP! Plus (as detailed below).

MAKEGEAR M2

Also just making it into our list of consumer 3D printers is the $1,499 MakerGear M2 (which is also available as a $1,299 kit). Like the Cube, this will print in both ABS and PLA

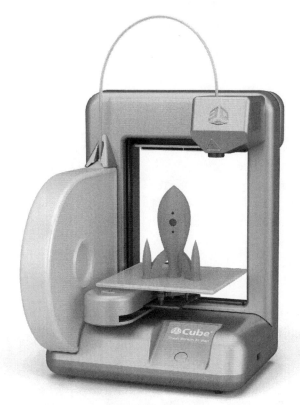

Figure 5.3: A Cube 3D Printer.
Image credit: 3D Systems Corporation.

(here supplied on a widely-available standard spool), and can be 'fed' digital designs on an SD card to allow printing without a computer.

The MakeGear M2 is derived from the RepRap Prussa Mendel design, and has a shiny, steel shell. Out of the box, the quality of printouts is generally reported to be good, with many opportunities existing to tweak things due to the MakeGear's open source heritage. Build volume is quite large (at about 200 x 250 x 200 mm, or 7.9 x 9.8 x 7.9 inches), allowing bigger things to be printed than with most of its competitors.

PORTABEE

As its name suggests, the Portabee 3D printer is designed to be easily transported. In fact, due to its clip-on/clip-off frame, this 2.8 kg piece of kit can be collapsed in seconds to fit into a laptop bag. As with most other models included here, the Portabee prints in both ABS and PLA thermoplastic filament supplied to it from a standard spool. Build volume is 120 x 120 x 120 mm (4.7 x 4.7 x 4.7 inches).

Aesthetically, the Portabee will not win any design awards. But it delivers the goods for $699 pre-assembled, or $499 as a kit. At under half the cost of a Cube or MakeGear M2, it is therefore a very serious contender as a real consumer model.

PRINTRBOTS

Printrbot is a company set up by a cool guy and former pastor called Brook Drum. A self-confessed 'maker', Brook found himself working in web design and wanted to get back to producing things that he could actually touch. The result was a range of 'Printrbots' – very distinctive, low-cost 3D printers with bodies made from laser-cut plywood.

To get his Printrbots into production, Brook set up a funding campaign on Kickstarter.com to raise $25,000. Pledges to this value were gained in 48 hours, with the final total raised in 30 days being $830,828. A year later all of those who had pledged money had received their Printrbots, and the company is thriving. Or as Brook cheerfully enthused when I interviewed him at the 3D Printshow in October 2012 'I'm Brook, I did a Kickstarter in November last year . . . and now I'm in the 3D printer business!'

OK, so what 3D printer models does Printrbot have on offer? Well, for $649 (or $499 as a kit) you can buy a Printrbot

LC. This has a 150 x 150 x 150 mm (5.9 x 5.9 x 5.9 inch) build volume, and prints in ABS and PLA. There is also a Printrbot Plus for $799 ($699 kit) with a 200 x 200 x 200 mm (7.9 x 7.9 x 7.9 inch) build volume, as well as my favourite, the Printrbot Junior. The latter is a small, foldable 3D printer with a 115 x 140 x 100 mm (4.5 x 5.5 x 4 inch) build volume. Out of the box, the Printrbot Junior can only print in PLA (as it does not have a heated build platform), but is priced down at $499 (or $399 as a kit). PLA is also a safer material to 3D print in than ABS, as it is entirely organic, with no toxic fumes ever emanating from the printer's print head as plastic melts.

The Printrbot range is not quite as easy to use as a Cube. But with a little patience the distinctive wooden-bodied printers can deliver excellent results. Reviews are also very positive. For example, *MAKE Magazine* have badged the Printrbot Junior 'Best in Class' as an entry level 3D printer. If I were going to spend $499 on a 3D printer I would buy a Printrbot Junior. Well OK, I would probably get the $399 kit, but the end result would hopefully be the same!

SOLIDOODLE

Another source of very-good-value consumer 3D printers is Solidoodle. This company offers fully-assembled, print-out-of-the-box models from $499 (for a base Solidoodle 2), $599 (for 'pro' model with a heated build platform), and $699 (for an 'expert' model with a better power supply, fully enclosed build area and internal lighting). All models feature a 150 x 150 x 150 mm (5.9 x 5.9 x 5.9 inch) build volume, with the base model best suited to printing in PLA, and the 'pro' and 'expert' printers capable of using both PLA and ABS. Like several other printers included here, Solidoodle has a RepRap heritage. Also like most other models, it may not be welcomed by everybody as an ideal addition to the lounge. Though as *MAKE Magazine* states,

Solidoodles are 'an absolute no-brainer for value-minded tinkerers'.

UP! & AFINIA

Finally in this round-up of 3D printers that real people may actually own, I give you two models from PP3DP, and one from Afinia. Confused? Well that is understandable. The thing is, the printers concerned – the $1,499 UP! Plus, $899 UP! Mini and $1,599 Afinia H Series – all come from the same manufacturer. And that manufacturer is neither UP!, PP3DP or Afinia, but the Beijing-based Delta Micro Factory Corporation. As I mentioned back in chapter 2, PP3DP is Delta Micro's US brand, while its printers are also imported into the US and re-badged by Afinia.

As will be immediately obvious to anybody who actually lays eyes on both, the UP! Plus and Afinia H Series are exactly the same printer. They are also rather good, no-frills hardware (if not for the tinkerer), and a solid rival to the 3D Systems Cube for those who do not mind a boxy painted metal frame as opposed to a curvy, designer plastic shell. As I said above, if I were going to spend c.$1,500 on a 3D printer, it would either be an UP! Plus or a Cube.

The UP! Plus/Afinia H Series has a build volume of 140 x 140 x 135 mm (5.5 x 5.5 x 5.3 inches), can print in ABS or PLA, and is a rather rugged thing. Its smaller buddy – the UP! Mini – achieves a smaller price tag by reducing its build volume to 120 x 120 x 120 mm (4.7 x 4.7 x 4.7 inches). It also has an entirely different, enclosed design and in many ways looks a lot more professional than its more expensive sibling.

AN INTERNET OF 3D-PRINTABLE THINGS

While a 3D printer is essential for anybody who wishes to fabricate stuff at home, it is clearly not the only thing that is required. In addition, all of those who choose to cohabit with a 3D printer will need digital object designs. These may be created from scratch (using software like SketchUp, Cubify Invent or Autodesk 123D), or perhaps captured using a 3D scanner. These options are, however, likely to remain relatively minority activities, with most 3D printed objects being downloaded from the Internet.

A growing number of websites allow for the upload, exchange and download of digital objects, and we should expect a lot more to pop-up very soon. This said, right now the clear frontrunner is Thingiverse. This was established by MakerBot Industries founders Zach Hoeken and Bre Pettis in 2008, and allows anybody to access and contribute to a 'universe of things'.

Over at thingiverse.com, Thingiverse describes itself as follows:

> Thingiverse is a place for you to share your digital designs with the world. We believe that just as computing shifted away from the mainframe into the personal computer that you use today, digital fabrication will share the same path. In fact, it is already happening: laser cutters, CNC machines, 3D printers, and even automated paper cutters are all getting cheaper by the day. These machines are useful for a huge variety of things, but you need to supply them with a digital design in order to get anything useful out of them. We're hoping that together we can create a community of people who create and share designs freely, so that all can benefit from them.

Thingiverse already contains tens of thousands of objects that in total have been downloaded over eight million times. The range of things on offer is also vast, and includes engagement rings, scanned human faces, dental braces, figurines, vehicle models, flying drones, photographic accessories, tablewares, shirt buttons and the obligatory mobile phone cases. Via the integrated 'MakerBot Customizer' app, Thingiverse even allows some objects to be customized before download. Already this allows people to tailor a range of designs to their own requirements, including skateboard wedges, spectacle frames, gears, pill boxes, bracelets and tool holders.

While Thingiverse is run by the founders of MakerBot Industries, the site can be used by anybody who wants to upload or download an object for fabrication on any 3D printer. So much is this the case that even designs incompatible with MakerBot printers are hosted. As co-founder Bre Pettis recently explained to *Forbes Magazine*:

> We keep it open because it feels right. There's no downside to sharing it. [Users of competitor 3D printers] are going to make stuff and share on Thingiverse, too, and that just benefits our community.

THE BIRTH OF OPEN DESIGN

If personal 3D printing at home ever does go truly mainstream, most people will either have to rely on sites like Thingiverse, or will need to pay to download digital object files. The latter is of course a possibility. But at present the rise of Thingiverse, and of personal fabrication more generally, seems to suggest that we may be entering a new era of 'open design'. This refers to the development of products through the use of publicly shared design information. Open designs are by definition free for anybody to download, adapt and 3D print, and may potentially take the 'information wants to be free' mentality of the early Internet into the physical realm.

For many decades we have been used to the designs of almost everything we own being closely-controlled intellectual property. To maintain this situation, corporate lawyers have been constantly primed to descend on springs at the first sign of anybody trying to infringe their company's patent. One only has to look at the constant lawsuits that plague the mobile phone and tablet industries to see the mess that over-zealous patenting has brought to that sector.

Critics of the potential spread of open design argue that it is likely to remain a niche and largely irrelevant activity as few people will ever have the ability, time or inclination to actually design their own stuff. The latter part of this argument may also be true – although many currently closet designers and inventors are likely to emerge from their cupboards as 3D printing allows more and more of their ideas to be physically manifested for real application. Even more significantly, even if few people are ever able to design stuff or want to do so, it is highly likely that lots of people will be keen to 3D print free designs once the technology to do this becomes cheap and reliable.

Ten years ago, almost all of the media content that most people consumed was created by for-profit organizations. Yet today, a significant proportion of the words, images, audio and video that most of us regularly devour are created for non-profit purposes by fellow citizens. Some of this media is private social content shared on sites like Facebook. But a reasonable quantity of widely-consumed audiovisual material is now crafted and provided for free in public arenas such as YouTube.

Given that the delivery of free content over the Internet is already a common reality, we ought to expect the provision of free, open design objects to become popular sooner rather than later. Granted, the design of free stuff for personal fabrication may raise all sorts of safety, security and legal issues.

But so too has our mass population of cyberspace, and most of us still seem to be surviving pretty well online.

HACKERSPACES, FABLABS & MAKERS

Other developments closely integrated with the rise of personal fabrication and open design are 'hackerspaces', 'FabLabs' and the broader 'Maker Movement'. These highly-similar initiatives all involve private individuals taking the means of design, production and repair into their own or community hands. None are a 3D printing development *per se*. But for most 'hackers', 'fabbers' and 'makers', 3D printers are a key weapon in their very practical armoury.

Hackerspaces and FabLabs may be broadly defined as open community workshops where members can share resources and knowledge to help them turn their ideas into physical reality. Many hackerspaces and all FabLabs are equipped with a variety of 3D printers and computer-controlled machine tools, with the FabLab Central website (at fab.cba.mit.edu) indicating a key element of any FabLab to be 'digital fabrication'.

Individual hackerspaces started life in Germany in the 1990s, with Hackerspaces.org set up by Paul Bohm and some other pioneering enthusiasts in 2007 to electronically link them together and to help the movement grow. Meanwhile, the FabLab (or 'Fabrication Laboratory') concept was created in 2003 by Dr. Neil Gershenfeld, Director of the Center for Bits and Atoms at the Massachusetts Institute of Technology (MIT).

To operate as a FabLab, a workshop has to provide public access to its facilities, to subscribe to the FabLab charter, to participate in the global FabLab network, and to share a common and quite extensive set of tools (which include 3D printers). Hackerspaces do not currently have such a formal list of common requirements, but very much share the same broad goal of democratizing the means of production within a local and global community.

According to the FabWiki (at wiki.fablab.is), at the time of writing there are 234 FabLabs operating in 52 countries. Meanwhile Hackerspaces.org lists over 500 active hackerspaces also spread right around the planet. Getting together on a community basis to share technology for personal fabrication is therefore certainly taking hold.

The above trend is also evidenced by the rise of the 'Maker Movement'. According to a neat posting by Cory Janssen on Technopedia.com, this may be defined as:

> . . . the name given to the increasing number of people employing do-it-yourself (DIY) and do-it-with-others (DIWO) techniques and processes to develop unique technology products. Generally, DIY and DIWO enables individuals to create sophisticated devices and gadgets, such as printers, robotics and electronic devices, using diagrammed, textual and/or video demonstration. With all the resources now available over the Internet, virtually anyone can create simple devices, which in some cases are widely adopted by users.

Unlike a hackerspace or FabLab, nobody has to join the Maker Movement. Rather, via their actions they may simply be identified as a 'maker' and part of it. All active members of hackerspaces and FabLabs – and indeed other 'makerspaces' – are likely to be 'makers', as are most people who currently own a low-cost 3D printer.

As Audrey Watters argued in November 2012 on Hack-Education.com, the Maker Movement now 'reflects the technological, political, and economic zeitgeist'. In 2011, *Wired* magazine even put a maker by the name of Lady Ada (who runs the online maker store Adafruit Industries) on its front cover. As a whole host of columnists have now written, in the last year or two the Maker Movement has gone from the margins to the mainstream to become a top technology trend. It is also no coincidence that this has happened concurrently with the rise of personal 3D printing.

In the United States there are now regular 'hackathons' and massive 'Maker Faires' to bring together members of the maker cause. The latter are run by *MAKE Magazine*, and according to Audrey Watters are 'a little bit science fair, a little bit hobbyist and hacker expo, and a whole lot of celebration of the DIY and "Maker" culture'. Just as computer geeks became cool during the PC and Internet revolutions (well, as least the successful ones!), so makers, hackers and fabbers are likely to see their street cred rise as a new age of personal fabrication takes hold.

BUREAU SOLUTIONS

In the introduction to the *MAKE Ultimate Guide to 3D Printing*, *MAKE Magazine* founder Dale Dougherty recalls a talk he made in New York University in September 2012. Dale was speaking mainly to undergraduate and postgraduate students, and asked how many owned a 3D printer. Not one person raised a hand. But when he asked how many of them *wanted* a 3D printer, every hand in the room went up.

The above is I guess not surprising. Not least due to recent sugar-glazed reports in the popular press, 3D printers are believed by many non-users to be magic devices that somehow conjure finished products out of thin air. At least at present, and as I hope this book has made abundantly clear, in most instances this is absolutely not the case. All consumer 3D printers, including the best-of-breed, $1,500 or less devices detailed in this chapter, may be amazing contraptions. But they have limited resolution, and only 3D print in a single thermoplastic build material. This still makes them potentially very useful devices. But a lot of the final products that people want are not made of plastic, and may not even be made from plastic in the future.

I suspect that many current and prospective 'makers', 'hackers' and 'fabbers' would gladly auction off some of their less immediately vital body parts just to have their own 3D printer at home. Such individuals would probably also be very happy with their purchase, and would probably introduce a plethora of wacky new plastic things into their local communities and close circle of family and friends. Nevertheless, I still strongly believe that, for a decade or more, 'personal fabrication' will be dominated by those in-store and online 3D printing bureaus that allow people who do not own a 3D printer to turn a digital design into a physical thing.

Back in chapter 3, I described the online printing services Shapeways, i.materialise and Sculpteo, as well as indicating the existence of many similar services. All of these are pretty easy to use, integrate well with high-end, low-end and free 3D modelling software, and provide anybody with access to high-end 3D printers based on all popular technologies. The price for getting an uploaded object 3D printed in plastic, metal, a ceramic or another material using one of these services is admittedly still rather high. But already it is far cheaper for people who just want to print a few things a year to use a bureau service than to invest in their own 3D printer. And this is before the benefits of having access to all available technologies are considered.

The key thing about the 3D Printing Revolution for most people will be that it will allow them to fabricate things they previously could not buy (and most probably by downloading and possibly tweaking an open design). Whether the printer that allows this to happen is located in their own home, their local FabLab or hackerspace, in a local store, or in a Shapeways or i.materialise factory, will matter far less than the possession of those final objects or components that get printed out. OK, so the first time you sit watching a 3D printer in operation it is pretty damn cool. But no sane individual sits staring at an inkjet or laser printer for hours on end as it does its stuff, and I strongly suspect that most people will get bored pretty quickly watching even the most amazing 3D printer. Many people will also realize this pre-purchase, avoid the capital outlay entirely, and instead opt to use bureau services when required. As we saw in the last chapter, plenty of direct digital manufacturing pioneers currently rely on online bureaus rather than their own hardware, and this should tell us a great deal.

DRIVING THE REVOLUTION

As we have seen in this chapter, it is now possible for at least some people to build their own, open source 3D printer, or to purchase relatively-low-cost, pre-assembled hardware. Digital object designs may then be freely downloaded from the Internet and either directly printed out or customized as desired. In addition to these amazing developments, FabLabs and hackerspaces now exist in which many people are free to innovate and experiment. 3D printing bureau services are additionally ready and waiting to turn anybody's digital design into a real, physical thing. It is therefore hardly surprising that so many now claim that we stand at the dawn of a New Age of free-for-all personal fabrication.

Like all great periods of industrial transition, the 3D Printing Revolution will be driven forward both by what individuals want to do, as well as by what we all more collectively need to do. The things we want to do may well involve personal fabrication at home, in store and online. Some such personal manufacture may also be undertaken by citizens wishing to escape the clutches of those large corporations who dominate consumer society in the early 21st century.

Beyond fulfilling individual desires to alter how our possessions are made, 3D printing may additionally play a critical role in helping human civilization to live more sustainably. A decade or two from now, the world is going to be very different from today, with more and more industrialized citizens demanding an increasing share of diminishing resources. To an increasing number of people this fact is patently obvious. And yet, some of those who evangelize about the forthcoming 3D Printing Revolution appear to ignore our inescapable challenges ahead. As a result, many 3D printing thought leaders continue to base their visions on a future world that they expect to be the same as today, if with widespread 3D printing added. Or in other words, they focus on how the 3D Printing Revolution will develop based solely on what people want to do, while ignoring what we will all collectively need to do.

To myself as a futurist, the above is at best somewhat daft, and at worst quite alarming. The wider context of the changing environment in which we live simply has to be a major factor that will determine how 3D printing will develop and enter mainstream application. In the next chapter I am therefore going to highlight some of the key challenges that the human race will soon need to address, and how 3D printing may help us to deal with them most successfully.

6
3D PRINTING & SUSTAINABILITY

Few new technologies arrive in isolation. Rather, the majority of new machines and processes are born within the context of their particular age, and this is certainly the case when it comes to 3D printing. Just when we are learning to accurately manufacture all manner of things in thin layers, so the world is waking up to the grand challenges of pending resource scarcity and climate change. We must therefore appraise the 3D Printing Revolution in this context.

In January 2012, a seminal report from the United Nations High Level Panel on Global Sustainability succinctly captured the essence of our situation. As it explained:

> The challenges we face are great, but so too are the new possibilities that appear when we look at old problems with new and fresh eyes. These possibilities include technologies capable of pulling us back from the planetary brink.

This chapter assesses how 3D printing may be one of the future technologies that could help us to live more sustainably. As in other chapters, my focus will largely be on real, practical developments that may showcase the way ahead. But just before we get to those, it is worth stepping back for a page or few to outline the major challenges on the relatively near horizon. For those who would like to be even better informed, you can read more in my 2012 books *Seven Ways to Fix the World* and *25 Things You Need to Know About the Future.*

OUR GRAND CHALLENGES AHEAD

The ecological footprint of the human race is already significantly beyond what the Earth can sustain, with the finite resource supplies of our first planet starting to be seriously depleted. To both avoid environmental catastrophe and to maintain our standard of living, within a few decades we will therefore need to start achieving more with less.

Almost certainly, the most immediate resource challenge on the medium-term horizon is 'Peak Oil'. This refers to the point in time when global oil production will reach its maximum, and after which demand for oil will start to outstrip supply. Exactly when Peak Oil will occur is a matter of heated debate, with some putting the date as early as 2015. To try and clarify matters, in 2009 the UK Energy Research Centre produced a report based on a review of 500 previous studies, as well as an analysis of major industry databases and 14 global oil supply forecasts. Their final document subsequently concluded that 'a peak in conventional oil production before 2030 appears likely and there is a significant risk of a peak before 2020'.

Given the reliance of our civilization on petroleum, the consequences of hitting Peak Oil will be extremely serious. For a start, around 50 per cent of oil is used to run vehicles. Part of the remainder then fuels other machinery and some power stations, with the rest used in the manufacture of a great many things. These include plastics, inorganic pesticides, pharmaceuticals, paints, fabrics such as nylon and polyester, and many other petrochemical compounds. Even the tarmac on our roads is produced from petroleum.

Unfortunately, oil is not the only critical resource whose availability is going to peak in the next decade or so. For example, as the United Nations has been warning for many years, fresh water supplies are also under threat, with 'Peak Water' on the imminent horizon in many parts of the world. Across the 20th century the quantity of fresh water tapped by the human race went up by a factor of nine, with about 50 per cent of fresh water now being diverted for human use. This level of usage is also well beyond what can be sustained in many regions, with the water table falling alarmingly in many parts of the world including China, India, the Middle East and the southern United States. As a consequence, the United Nations believes that 'by 2025, 1.8 billion people will be living in countries or regions with absolute water scarcity, and two-thirds of the world's population could be living under water stressed conditions'.

In part as a consequence of looming constraints in oil and water supply, global food shortages are likely to become both increasingly common and more intense. In many developed nations, every calorie of food delivered to our plates requires about ten calories of oil to be consumed to produce pesticides, to run farm machinery, and to transport, refine and package our daily bread. A decrease in the availability of petroleum (or a significant increase in its price) will therefore reduce food production levels. In addition, globally about 30 per cent of agricultural land is now suffering falling productivity due to soil erosion and over-intensive farming methods. Fish stocks around the planet are additionally in decline, with the 2010 *Census of Marine Life* reporting that commercial fishing on a global scale will collapse entirely by 2050 unless drastic action is taken.

Many scientists believe that food production is also under threat due to climate change. Rising temperatures have now been pretty clearly linked to water shortages and soil erosion, and in turn to decreasing crop yields. Indeed, it is estimated that 2°C of global warming – the minimum now believed realistically possible this century – will reduce grain yields across southern Europe by 20 per cent, have a similar impact on rice production in Asia, and could result in the extinction of up to 40 per cent of species on the planet. Such a level of warming is also expected to flood land that is currently home to 1 person in 20, as well as leading to more extreme weather conditions with related property damage and crop failures.

In addition to climate-related issues and future shortages of oil, water and food, broader resource depletion is a future physical certainty. The materials available on Planet Earth are by definition finite, and we are using them up at an increasingly alarming rate. Again to cite United Nations figures (this time from its Environment Programme), if nothing is done humanity's demand for natural resources will rise to around 140 billion tonnes of minerals, ores, fossil fuels and biomass every year by 2050. This compares to about 50 billion tonnes in 2010. You do not have to be a resource scientist to understand that an almost three-fold increase in the use of finite planetary resources is not remotely sustainable. Inevitably, therefore – and as I said at the start of this overview – in the relatively near future we all have to start achieving more with less.

EMPOWERING LOCALIZATION

The previous section highlighted just some of the critical issues that we will fairly soon need to address. There are of course many other future challenges that we will not be able to ignore – including ongoing austerity, debt reduction, population ageing and population expansion – but I do not want to get us too depressed! While reporting some alarming research and statistics, the United Nations and others do thankfully remind us that new technologies and altered modes of living offer considerable hope for a prosperous, more sustainable future. And, returning to the focus of this book, 3D printing looks exceedingly likely to prove part of the solution rather than part of the problem.

One of the first major benefits of the 3D Printing Revolution will be the opportunities it raises for 'localization'. Since the beginning of the Industrial Revolution, we have increasingly relied on complex production technologies that have had to be centralized far away from where most people live. While for many centuries this meant producing things a few tens or hundreds of miles from their point of sale, since the 1980s humanity has become obsessed with globalization. As a consequence, today a great many things are produced thousands of miles from the place we buy them. So much is this the case that today about one sales dollar in seven is spent on transportation. For narrow-minded economists and corporate accountants who do not factor diminishing oil supplies and climate change into their theories and ledgers, this current state of affairs is not a problem. But whether they and others like it or not, within a decade or so globalization is going to have to give way at least partially to localization.

As we have seen in earlier chapters, 3D printers are multipurpose devices that may be used to manufacture things on a very local basis, and sometimes even at home. A 3D printer may potentially never even make the same product or component twice, so allowing local businesses to become highly effective Jacks and Jills of all trades. A few decades hence, broad-market local businesses with 3D printing facilities may therefore be able to meet a wide range of local customer requirements just as traditional craftspeople always did in the pre-industrial age. Our current 'requirement' to import so many goods from overseas nations will therefore diminish.

DIGITAL STORAGE & TRANSPORTATION

As the local manufacture of products using 3D printers becomes more widespread, so the 'digital transportation' of many items will become a greater and greater possibility. Moving around bits of digital information is also more environmentally friendly than shipping physical things made from atoms. A very few companies – such as Freedom of Creation – have already embraced the idea of at least partial digital transportation, with their high-end designer products 'shipped' over the Internet and 3D printed in a facility as close as possible to their customer's final location. When we purchase something from a website in the future, we may therefore no longer receive a parcel from UPS, but instead a set of print-rights and a password that will allow us to 'materialize' our purchase at the 3D printing bureau closest to our home.

Just as significant as digital object transportation will be digital object storage, as this may end excessive overproduction. The current industrial model of remote mass production dictates that many things are manufactured in considerable bulk in the hope that a future purchaser will exist. Unfortunately, in many cases this turns out to be exceedingly wasteful, with many manufactured products never actually getting sold. Even when every item produced in a factory does find an owner, it often spends a considerable proportion of its early life in a range of storage facilities that inevitably consume precious energy and other resources. Environmentally, it is essential that every item we make enters useful application as soon as possible after it is made, and local 3D-print-on-demand could help in making this a common future reality.

A RETURN TO PRODUCT REPAIR

Another key benefit of digital object storage and local manufacture is likely to be increased product repair. Over the
past half century most people in developed economies have
become obsessed with constant product replacement, rather
than the long-term maintenance of possessions to which we
may become emotionally attached.

Most of our grandparents or great-grandparents saved for
long periods to purchase products that they kept for life. In
stark contrast, many people today borrow to buy goods that
are sometimes discarded before they are even paid for. Such
a state of affairs is neither individually desirable or
environmentally sustainable. Fairly soon we must therefore
return to an age in which we mend and upgrade things that
are no longer operative or fit for purpose, rather than casually
throwing them away.

Today, one of the main reasons that so many nearly-
functional items end up in landfill is that very few products
have replaceable parts. This is due to both poor product
design, as well as the fact that most manufacturers would
prefer us to sell us a new product rather than helping us to
repair a broken one. These points noted, even when product
repair is championed, it usually proves uneconomic for
companies to make all possible spare parts available at the
right times in the right locations.

Widespread, local 3D printing will change the repairability
landscape, with spare parts for most products able to be stocked
digitally and manufactured-on-demand. Even when a spare
part cannot be tracked down online, enterprising individuals
(or future repair bureau) will be able to either design a new part
from scratch, or to scan a broken item, repair it digitally in a
computer, and print out a replacement. As Jay Leno recently
explained in *Popular Mechanics*, when he needs a spare part for
a 100 year old car, he already just scans and 3D prints.

By itself, the ability to make spare parts will be insufficient to get things mended, as skilled people (or robots!) will be required to open up broken possessions and fit replacement 3D printed components. Though, as we saw in the last chapter, the 'Maker Movement' is on the rise, with an increasing number of people keen to take responsibility for producing and maintaining their own stuff. This also only represents a return to a fairly recent bygone age. Only a few decades back, when a kettle or electric fire stopped working most people went to the hardware store, purchased a new element, and fitted it themselves. One of the most obvious ways to achieve more with less is not for everybody to have less stuff, but for us all to keep the stuff we have for longer. By facilitating increased product repair, the 3D Printing Revolution should also allow this to happen.

IMPROVED MATERIAL UTILIZATION

Another key environmental benefit of widespread 3D printing will be a more effective utilization of increasingly scarce resources. Today, many industrial processes consume vast quantities of raw materials that never end up as part of a final product. This is because many current production methods are subtractive. In other words, they start with a solid block of material and then cut, lathe, file, drill and otherwise remove bits from it. In contrast, 3D printers start with nothing and only add on the material that the final object requires.

Reducing materials wastage will reduce costs as well as making things more sustainable. For both of these reasons, some major manufacturers are already seriously investigating the possibilities for direct digital manufacture. For example, Rolls-Royce is leading a project called MERLIN. This is being funded by the European Union, and is working toward the use of 3D printing in the manufacture of civil aircraft engines. Using direct metal laser sintering (DMLS) and related 3D printing technologies, the hope is to achieve close to a 100 per cent utilization of raw materials in engine manufacture

The potential material and cost savings may also be very considerable indeed. For example, as a Rolls-Royce engineer told me a couple of years ago, today a typical one tonne aircraft engine is produced from about 6.5 tonnes of metal. Most of this ends up on the machine shop floor, with a great deal of it being a high-priced metal like titanium. By transitioning to the 3D printing of aircraft components, a material saving in the order of up to 80 per cent may therefore be achieved, yet with exactly the same final product being produced.

Another benefit of direct digital manufacturing using 3D printers is the potential to create less dense final parts that weigh less. Once again those with an interest in aeroplane manufacture are taking the lead, as lighter components could result in more energy-efficient aircraft. The airline industry has set itself an ambitious target to reduce its carbon emissions by 50 percent by 2050. It is therefore hardly surprising that aerospace manufacturers are intent on investigating the potential of 3D printing as one means of achieving this goal.

For example, at the EADS Innovation Works near Bristol in the United Kingdom, experiments are taking place producing small parts for the Airbus A380 airliner using DMLS. The first such part produced was a new hinge for a jet engine cover. This has been designed to do exactly the same job as a conventional component, but uses only half as much metal. This startling result has been achieved via a redesign that removes bulk from the hinge where it is not structurally required. The resultant new component could not easily (let alone cost effectively) be produced using traditional tooling, but is straightforward to manufacture using a 3D printer.

EADS Innovation Works is currently subjecting its first DMLS components to structural testing, and hopes that successful results will allow it to scale up to 3D print far larger aircraft components that will save a great deal of weight and metal. These include the spar beams that support airliner wings.

A similar initiative called the SAVING Project equally has the intention of creating more sustainable products using 3D printing. Standing for 'Sustainable product development via design optimization and AdditiVe manufacturING), this was established in September 2009 and is funded by the United Kingdom's Technology Strategy Board. As the SAVING website at manufacturingthefuture.co.uk explains:

> The project aims to develop lightweight and sustainable products via material design optimization and additive manufacturing (AM) which will significantly save materials and energy consumption in the production of high value products. As an innovative and promising material process technology, AM allows the rapid development of sustainable products through new lightweight material structure technology that utilises functional metal and plastic materials more effectively. It has the potential to produce high value aerospace, medical and engineering parts with minimum material waste and energy input. For certain complex parts, AM [technology] can save up to 90% of the material compared to subtractive machining processes.

Much of the work of the SAVING project is directed toward using 3D printing to design and create industrial components with 'previously impossible geometries'. For example, via design optimization, final metal parts may be manufactured that feature hollow or cellular (honeycombed) internal structures that would be impossible to achieve either by machining a block of material, or when creating a final part by pouring metal or injecting plastic into a mold.

Like MERLIN, the SAVING project has already demonstrated the feasibility of its intent, with many highly impressive case studies included on its website. One of these reports on work by Plunkett Associates to design and 3D print a simple aerospace bell crank that uses a reduced volume of material. The result is a part identical in functionality to one traditionally machined from aluminium, but 21 per cent lighter.

Another case reports on work by Crucible Industrial Design to create a lighter seat buckle for commercial passenger jets. While initially the benefits of doing this may appear to be negligible, the finished buckle created by Crucible (a beautiful item laser sintered in titanium) weights just 70 grams. With a conventional steel buckle weighing 155 grams, this means a saving of 85 grams per buckle, which would compound to a 72.5 kg saving for all of the 853 seat buckles used on an Airbus A380. Given that a weight reduction of just 1 kg can save 45,000 litres of fuel over the lifetime of a large passenger plane, new buckles produced using DMLS could stop about 3.3 million litres of aviation fuel from being burnt. At current oil prices, this would save about £2 million in the life of an aircraft (and far more as we approach Peak Oil). The cost of 3D printing a plane load of seat buckles in titanium (estimated at £165,000 using current technology) would therefore easily be compensated for, in addition to the positive environmental impact of the plane burning less fuel.

Potential savings resulting from direct digital manufacturing will also not be limited to the production of new vehicle components. As we saw in chapter 4, in the future it is quite possible that buildings (or parts thereof) will be 3D printed, again with materials added to the construction only where absolutely necessary. Homes or workplaces 3D printed in extruded concrete or binder-jetted sand will even be able to feature air gaps and honeycomb shapes within their walls, roofs and floors that will not just reduce weight, but additionally improve the building's insulation. As Cameron Naramore argued on 3DPrinter.net in November 2012, due to reduced materials usage, greater materials uniformity, more control over design, and other factors, 'future buildings will be markedly more efficient than the drafty boxes we currently call homes'. As Cameron went on to explain:

> Building houses out of lumber and nails requires constructing temporary scaffolding that's often not reusable; the scaffolds of future houses will be the printers themselves and will simply be transported from one construction site to the next and [will build] no more than what will be lived in, which further reduces logistics. Walls printed in one material will be more efficient than the concrete, wood, fiberglass, and plaster we sandwich together now because they'll be seamless, multiporous, and of complex geometries specially designed to keep the weather outside.

MATERIAL RECYCLING

Turning our attention from high-end industrial to domestic 3D printing, some people are becoming concerned about the cost and availability of the filament used in thermoplastic extrusion. The majority of 3D printers do, after all, currently make plastic objects, and usually these build materials are made from petroleum. As Peak Oil looms, we therefore need to find new sources of plastic filament, or at least to utilize the plastic we have as efficiently as possible.

In an attempt to address the matter, a young inventor called Tyler McNaney has created 'Filabot'. As illustrated in figure 6.1. this is a 'plastic reclaimer' that can turn waste plastics – including old 3D printouts – into brand new 3D printing filament. As the filabot.com website further explains:

> Filabot is a desktop extruding system, capable of grinding various types of plastics, to make spools of plastic filament for 3D printers. Not only is it user friendly, but it is also environmentally friendly. The Filabot can process things such as milk jugs, soda bottles, various other types of plastics, and [old or bad 3D printouts] to make new filament . . . Filabot will bring the real power of sustainability to 3D printing, allowing for a one stop shop to make anything.

Filabot consists of a grinder, an extruder and a spooling system. The grinder rips apart waste plastics, allowing chunks 'up to a good 3 x 3 inches' to be broken down. Once waste plastics have been ground up they can either be stockpiled, or fed into the Filabot extruder. Here they are melted and forced at pressure through a die to create a standard 3 or 1.75 mm 3D printing filament. After cooling, the Filabot spooling system automatically winds the filament onto a spool.

Owners of a Filabot can literally go to their trash, find some discarded plastic, and get it ground up and reformed into a 3D printing consumable that can be fed to their RepRap, MakerBot, Printrbot or other thermoplastic extrusion 3D printer. Or in other words, Filabot allows new

Figure 6.1: The Filabot Plastic Reclaimer.
Photograph reproduced with the permission of its inventor, Tyler McNaney. For more information see filabot.com.

objects to be 3D printed out of rubbish – or for old or failed 3D printouts to be recycled into something new.

Given the brilliance of the Filabot concept, I would not be at all surprised to see consumer 3D printers with integrated plastic reclaimers on the market well before the end of the decade. The opportunity to produce a machine that can take in waste and turn it into a custom product is just too significant not to become a common reality. In fact, on an industrial scale, this has already started to take place.

For example, a Dutch designer called Dirk Vander Kooij has managed to reprogram an old industrial robot to take scrap plastic from old refrigerators and to extrude it into tables and chairs. This low-resolution form of 3D printing outputs object layers in a plastic bead about 1 cm in diameter, and can produce a full-size, highly-durable chair in just three hours. Once again the potential to use 3D printing to help create products from recycled materials is demonstrated.

COMPLEMENTARY TECHNOLOGIES

Just as the 3D Printing Revolution will happen in a particular environmental context, so it is also beginning just as several other new technologies are coming to the fore. Many of these will also prove highly complementary to 3D printing and its development. For example, advancements in nanotechnology (the science of measuring and manufacturing on a close-to-atomic scale) are accruing rapidly, and could allow the benefits of 3D printing to be reaped across a wider and wider range of applications. Not least an experimental nanotech 3D printing technology called two-photon polymerization (2PP) is already in the lab. As we saw in chapter 2, this may increase the accuracy of stereolithography by 250 times, as well as significantly increasing its speed.

3D printing may also accrue benefits from developments in the very new science of synthetic biology. This involves the design and construction of entirely new living things using standardized genetic components called 'biobricks'. In May 2010, the J. Craig Venter Institute (JCVI) used such techniques to create the first ever entirely synthetic life form. Termed 'JCVI-syn1.0', this self-replicating, single-cell organism was based on an existing *Mycoplasma capricolum* bacterium. Yet, at its core was an entirely synthetic genome constructed from 1.08 million DNA base pairs in the JCVI laboratory.

So what has synthetic biology got to do with 3D printing? Well, already several companies – including Amyris, Joule Fuels, LS9 and OPX Biotechnologies – have begun to use synthetic biology to create synthetic micro-organisms that can turn organic materials into petrochemical substitutes including biofuels and bioacrylics. Most significantly for 3D printing, a team from the Korea Advanced Institute of Science & Technology have managed to use synthetic biology to create a synthetic micro-organism that can produce the bioplastic polylactic acid (PLA) from an organic feedstock such as corn, sugar cane or algae.

As we have seen in other chapters, PLA can already be used as a consumable in many thermoplastic extrusion 3D printers. Today this organic, biodegradable material is produced using a two-stage process that first ferments agricultural ingredients to produce lactic acid. A second, post-processing stage is then needed to polymerize the short lactic acid molecules into long polymer chains. However, the Korean team's work negates the need for this second, highly industrial process, so opening up the opportunity for PLA to be fermented locally in any location.

What the above means in practice is that, fairly soon, companies or even private individuals may be able to ferment old food, human excrement or animal waste directly into PLA that could then be 3D printed into plastic products or components. Alternatively, algae may be cultivated in large vats as a food stock from which PLA would be fermented using synthetic micro-organisms. In the relatively near future, people could even grow PLA foodstocks in their gardens, or hydroponically on their windowsills. As I argued in *25 Things You Need to Know About the Future*, a decade hence the potential exists not just to locally 3D print many products and components, but to do so from organic plastics that are fermented from biological materials also produced on a very local basis.

PART OF THE SOLUTION

As we have seen in this chapter, 3D printing may have an important role to play in helping us to become more enviromentally friendly. OK, so by itself 3D printing is not going to suddenly make our lives or economy more sustainable. Nevertheless, it is poised to radically alter how we make and maintain at least *some* products in a future world in which we will have to consume things less and value things more. Used appropriately with a mix of complementary technologies, 3D printing may indeed – as the United Nations hopes – help to 'pull us back from the planetary brink'.

By empowering localization and allowing us to rely more on the storage and communication of bits, and less on the transportation of atoms, 3D printing will undoubtedly assist with our transition to a post-Peak Oil mode of civilization. By decreasing materials wastage, optimising materials utilization and increasing opportunities for product repair, 3D printing will also help humanity to consume fewer metals and other increasingly scarce resources. In addition, by facilitating the construction of more energy efficient homes and vehicles, 3D printing will not only allow us to save energy, but to decrease our carbon footprint and so lessen the extent of climate change. Measures to mitigate climate change may also be assisted by the use of 3D printing in the manufacture of solar panels and other alternative energy infrastructure.

What I have not mentioned above are any potential ways in which 3D printing will help with the very pressing future challenges of Peak Water and global food shortages. Here I can only suggest that, by allowing us to save some of the fuel, energy and materials that we currently require for transportation and product manufacture, 3D printing will allow a greater balance of resources to be directed into food production. Some current 3D printing thought leaders – such as Hod Lipman, the author of the book *Fabricated* – argue that some future 3D printers will be able to output synthetic food and so potentially assist with future food shortages. Yet, as I will explain in depth in chapter 8, with this particular piece of future-gazing I wholeheartedly disagree.

A SUSTAINABLE COMMUNITY

When planning this book I was in two minds about including a chapter on 3D printing and sustainability. Personally, as you have probably gathered, I have a passion for this kind of stuff. I am, however, also aware that not everyone believes in climate change, let alone in any broader need to find ways to achieve more with less. Adding in 5,000 words on this topic was hence a difficult judgement call to make.

Ultimately, the reason that this chapter actually got written was due to the passion for sustainability that I encountered when conducting my interviews with 3D printing pioneers. I did not set out to ask anybody about how 3D printing may help to make human activities more sustainable. Even so, the potential for 3D printing to reap energy and material savings, to facilitate increased product repair, and to empower responsible 'makers', did come up fairly regularly. To me at least, it is therefore clear that many of the pioneers of the 3D Printing Revolution care pretty passionately about sustainability, and I subsequently felt it important to reflect that here.

Whether or not you are a 'sustainability convert', you hopefully by now agree that 3D printing has a strong chance of presenting humanity with a world of fresh opportunity. And if this does turn out to be the case, we would surely be crazy not to try and craft that new world to be more sustainable than the world of today.

7

BIOPRINTING

On the 3rd of March 2011, surgeon and regenerative medicine pioneer Anthony Atala gave a talk at the annual TED conference in California. Like all TED talks, Atala's presentation was video recorded and make freely available on the Internet via TED.com. Two years later, it had been watched over 800,000 times, and continues to be lauded as one of the best 'technology, entertainment, design' or 'TED' talks ever made.

In his presentation, Atala explained the increasing health crisis that is arising as people live longer and organ failure becomes more common. In the United States alone, up to 100,000 people are always waiting for an organ transplant, with this number roughly doubling every decade. Unfortunately, against this backdrop, the number of organs available for transplant is hardly increasing, with less than a third of those desiring an organ transplant ever receiving one. In response to this situation, Anthony Atala is one of a handful of pioneers who are working to create living, artificial human organs in the laboratory.

Anthony Alata is Director of the Wake Forest Institute for Regenerative Medicine in Winston-Salem, NC. Here researchers continue to make incredible progress in the field of artificial organ engineering. Not least, since 1999 several human bladders have been grown in their laboratory by seeding a scaffold with a culture of human cells. These bladders have then been successfully transplanted into patients who continue to live healthily. In his 2011 TED talk, Atala was even reunited with a young man for whom he had grown a new bladder a decade earlier.

Also in his talk, Atala demonstrated on stage a special 3D printer that was building a prototype human kidney. Such experimental artificial organs are still far from being ready to implant into human patients. Even so, when Atala held in his surgically-gloved hand a complete kidney that he had 'printed out earlier', his audience was understandably both shocked and amazed.

The so-termed 'bioprinting' of replacement human organs is without doubt the most radical application of 3D printing so far conceived. Bioprinting also happens to be the aspect of 3D printing to which I have devoted more attention than any other, and where I have had the most contact with those driving the technology forward.

By pure coincidence, around the time that Anthony Atala made his famous TED talk, I realized that very few people had created still images or video materials to illustrate the significant opportunity that bioprinting presents. I therefore undertook a personal project that resulted in conceptual bio-printing media that have become very popular, and which I have supplied and adapted for the use of several research teams and publications. Just one of my creations is the illus-tration of a future bioprinter shown in figure 7.1. If you are a 3D printing enthusiast you may well have seen this picture before. Though you probably had no idea that I created it!

In this chapter I am going to showcase the work of several pioneers who are striving to turn the bioprinting of human tissue into an everyday medical reality. As we shall see, within a few decades it may well be possible to bioprint re-

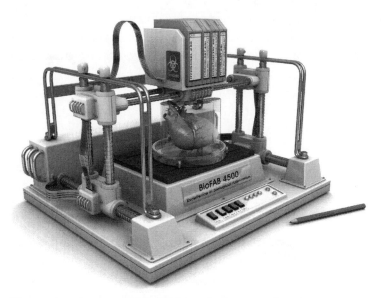

Figure 7.1: Concept Illustration of a Future Bioprinter.
Image created by Christopher Barnatt, ExplainingTheFuture.com.

placement arteries, kidneys, livers, pancreases and even hearts for routine transplant. Once the technology to achieve this has been appropriately developed, doctors may even start to heal wounds by bioprinting new cells directly onto their patients. In turn, this could allow bioprinting to transform not just how we heal the injured and the sick, but also the practice of cosmetic surgery.

FROM PHOTO PRINTER TO BIOPRINTER

Around the turn of the millennium, a Japanese paediatrician called Makoto Nakamura was becoming increasingly concerned about the number of his patients desperate for an organ transplant. He therefore started to investigate the possibility of creating mechanical, inorganic prosthetics. Then, quite by chance, Nakamura realised that the droplets of ink emitted from the print head in a standard inkjet photo printer are about the same size as human cells. The idea therefore dawned on him of turning a photo printer into a 3D bioprinter that could be loaded with a culture of human cells. The printer could then, at least in theory, output the cells via a material jetting process that would result in artificial, living tissue.

In 2002 Nakamura began his first experiments with a standard Epson photo printer. When initially loaded with cells, the device's print head simply clogged up. Undeterred, Nakamura made one of the strangest customer support calls in history! Fortunately, somebody at Epson was eventually receptive to his ideas, and with their assistance a year later he managed to use a modified photo printer to successfully output cells that survived the inkjet printing process. This was achieved by encasing the cells in sodium alginate to stop them from drying out, and by jetting them into a calcium-chloride solution.

Between April 2005 and March 2008, Makoto Nakamura led a bioprinting project at the Kanagawa Science and Technology Academy. Here he guided a team that scratch-built an experimental bioprinter. This was then used to create 'biotubing' from layers of two different types of cells, with about 15 mm of 1 mm diameter material output every minute. In a few years, such biotubing may be able to be used as a living replacement for human blood vessels. Far further into the future, Nakamura's hope is to be able to bioprint replacement organs for human transplant.

In addition to Professor Nakamura, several other researchers have managed to adapt standard inkjet printer mechanisms to demonstrate proof-of-concept bioprinting. Perhaps most notably, both Thomas Boland and Vladimir Mironov have each successfully conducted similar experiments. As long ago as September 2004, the First International Workshop on Bioprinting and Biopatterning was held at the University of Manchester in the UK. Since that time this annual event has brought together an increasing number of physicists, biologists and physicians all keen to push forward the boundaries of tissue engineering.

NATURE LENDS A HAND

Alongside Nakamura, Boland and Mironov, another highly significant bioprinting pioneer is Gabor Forgacs from the University of Missouri. In 1996, and following a painstaking study of chicken embryos, Forgacs recognised that cells stick together during embryonic development in a manner that could greatly assist in artificial tissue fabrication. By 2004, Forgacs had used this insight to start developing his own bioprinting technology. This builds tissues not from individually jetted cells, but by extruding 'clumps' of many thousands of cells. These clumps are technically termed 'bio-ink spheroids', and are injected into a water-based 'bio-paper' by a tiny, needle-like print head.

To advance his work, in 2007 Forgacs founded a company called Organovo with a mission to 'create tissue on demand for research and surgical applications'. By March 2008, Organovo had developed a bioprinter that was custom-made for them by microelectronics manufacturer nScrypt. Forgacs and his team then used this prototype to print both functional blood vessels and cardiac tissue using cells obtained from a chicken. Seventy hours after printout, the cells in the latter fused together so completely that they started beating.

In the next phase of their research, Organovo partnered with medical equipment manufacturer Invetech to create the NovoGen MMX. This was the world's first commercial bioprinter, and like Organovo's earlier prototype has multiple print heads. The first of these is loaded with bio-ink spheroids, while a second outputs a bio-paper support structure made from water mixed with gelatine, collagen or another hydrogel. The first NovoGen MMX was delivered to Organovo's lab in January 2009. At the time of writing, a further nine have been manufactured, each with a price tag of several hundred thousand dollars.

The NovoGen MMX bioprinting process first requires a sample of cells to be sourced from a patient biopsy or stem cells. These are then grown in the lab using standard biotech methods, before being cultured in a growth medium to create the required final volume of cells. All of the different cell types needed to create the tissue or organ to be printed are then mixed together into an aggregate. For example, if a blood vessel is to be bioprinted, an aggregate is created containing a mix of primary endothelial cells (which form the lining of blood vessels), smooth muscle cells (which allow blood vessels to expand and contract) and fibroblasts (which form tough connective tissue). This cell aggregate is then put into a cell-packing device that compresses and extrudes it like a kind of bio-ink sausage. An 'aggregate cutter' then chops this sausage into bits, with the very tiny pieces spontaneously forming into bio-ink spheroids that each contain between 10,000 and 30,000 individual cells.

Once an adequate supply of bio-ink spheroids have been loaded into a NovoGen MMX, the bioprinting process can begin in earnest. As shown in figure 7.2, initially a single layer of bio-paper is laid out by the NovoGen's first print head. The second print head then injects bio-ink spheroids into this bio-paper support. Additional layers of bio-paper and bio-ink spheroids are then alternately added to build up a three dimensional tissue structure.

Once initial 3D printout is complete, an amazing natural process takes place, with the bio-ink spheroids slowly fusing together into solid tissue as shown in the lower portion of figure 7.2. Quite staggeringly, not only do the individual cells fuse, but in addition they even rearrange to end up in the correct anatomical location. So, for example, the endothelial cells from the bio-ink aggregate migrate to the inside of a bioprinted blood vessel, while the smooth muscle cells move to the middle and the fibroblasts shift to the outside. In more complex bioprinted materials, intricate capillaries and other internal structures also form naturally. During this 'maturation phase' – or shortly after it has completed – the bio-paper that initially supported the non-fused cells either dissolves away or is otherwise removed.

The way in which clumps of cells can fuse together and rearrange after printout may sound almost magical. After all, once you have 3D printed an object using thermoplastic extrusion or stereolithography, you do not expect it to evolve and improve. And yet this is exactly what happens after a NovoGen MMX has done its stuff. While this may initially bewilder most people, as Gabor Forgacs explains, it is no different to the cells in an embryo knowing how to configure into complicated organs. Nature has been evolving this capability for billions of years. Once positioned in roughly the right places, appropriate cell types somehow just know what to do.

TOWARD TISSUE-ON-DEMAND

In December 2010, Organovo used a NovoGen MMX to create the first bioprinted human blood vessels. In April 2013 it even reported the successful bioprinting of human liver tissue. The company has also already successfully implanted nerve grafts into rats, and has the long-term goal of being able to produce tissues for human transplantation. Initially such on-demand printouts may be heart muscle patches, nerve grafts or sections of arteries, as these will be relatively small and simple to print, as well as being more likely to progress fairly rapidly through clinical trials.

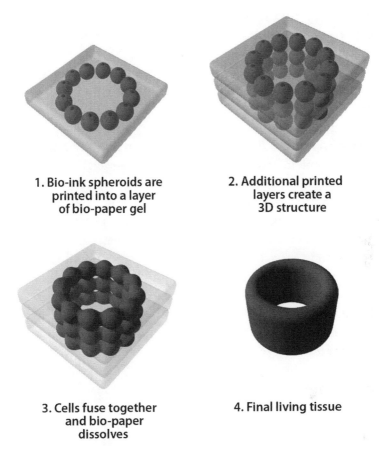

1. Bio-ink spheroids are printed into a layer of bio-paper gel

2. Additional printed layers create a 3D structure

3. Cells fuse together and bio-paper dissolves

4. Final living tissue

Figure 7.2: Bioprinting with Tissue Spheroids.

Once bioprinted patches and grafts enter clinical practice, so the foundation will have been laid for the eventual replacement of entire soft-tissue organs like kidneys or livers. This said, all of the potential human transplant applications of Organovo's technology remain some way into the future, with trials of the simplest soft-tissues probably at least five years away, and first implantation of even a 'simple' bio-printed organ like a kidney unlikely to occur until the late 2020s.

Given the above, in the short- and medium-term Organovo hopes to help pharmaceutical companies to speed the development of new drugs. Worldwide, trials of next generation medicines are increasingly failing, with innovative pharmaceutical compounds that worked fine in the lab very frequently not living up to expectation in animal or clinical trials. To help with this situation, the first commercial application of Organovo's technology is going to involve the production of bioprinted human tissues for pharmaceutical R&D. This will allow drug developers to test far more of their inventions at an early stage. Such tests will also be more likely to mimic the results of clinical trials than traditional lab tests or animal experiments. They may therefore save a great deal of time and money in drug development.

As just one example of a work-in-progress, in January 2013 Organovo formed a collaboration with the Knight Cancer Institute at Oregon Health & Science University (OHSU). As explained by Joe W. Gray from the OHSU, 'a major challenge in oncology research today is that animal models cannot accurately represent human physiology, and [cancer cells grown in the lab] do not provide information on how cells act in a three-dimensional, native architecture'. By developing bioprinted cancers and potentially other diseased tissue models, Organovo and the OHSU therefore hope to improve the understanding of new drug toxicity and efficacy far earlier in the pharmaceutical development process. In turn, this should allow safer, more effective therapies to be produced more rapidly and at lower cost.

In an entirely different kind of development, in December 2012 Organovo announced that it was working with Autodesk to create the first 3D design software for bioprinting.

This is intended to improve bioprinting usability and functionality by opening up access to the NovoGen MMX to a far wider range of users. Or as Organovo chairman Keith Murphy explained, his company's new relationship with Autodesk will offer 'the potential long-term ability for customers to design their own 3D tissues for production by Organovo'. While today a sculptor may upload a new piece of jewelry to Shapeways or i.materialise to 3D print in plastic or metal, tomorrow a doctor may send a digital model of an arterial graft or even an entire organ to Organovo for bioprintout and return by FedEx.

As all of the above hopefully makes clear, Organovo is a bioprinting company with realistic and well-founded short-, medium- and long-term goals. In 2012, the *MIT Technology Review* listed Organovo as one of the world's 50 most innovative companies, while in 2010 *Time Magazine* heralded the NovoGen MMX as one of its best inventions of that year. As you may remember from chapter 3, Organovo is already a publicly traded company, and one of only five 3D printer manufacturers of any genre to have this status. For anybody interested in the future of 3D printing, let alone bioprinting, Organovo therefore has to be a pioneer to watch.

CHALLENGES AHEAD

Another research team that is striving to make the bioprinting of human organs a future reality is based at the Advanced Tissue Biofabrication Center at the Medical University of South Carolina (MUSC). This research hub was in part established by Vladimir Mironov, and has developed a range of bioprinting and related hardware. Such devices include their Palmetto bioprinter and the DynaGen Bioreactor. The latter provides mechanical stimulation to artificially created tissues in order to improve their growth after maturation. As we all know, muscles are strengthened as a result of exercise, and bioprinted muscle is no different. Any future bioprinted heart will therefore have to be given a significant workout in the lab by an appropriate machine before it is strong enough to pump blood around a human body.

Another centre of excellence is the Biomanufacturing Laboratory at the University of Iowa. Here Dr. Ibrahim Ozbolat and his colleagues are working to try and make bioprinted organs for human transplant that can be 'fabricated at the click of a button'. And while, as elsewhere, great progress is being made, significant challenges also remain.

In a recent article in the *Industrial Engineer*, Dr Ozbolat outlined some of the key hurdles that need to be overcome. These include bioprinting organs that will function correctly, as well as the developments in stem cell technology necessary to isolate and culture appropriate build materials. Top of Ibrahim's immediate list, however, were the challenges associated with thick tissue fabrication. As he explained:

> Systems must be developed to transport nutrients, growth factors and oxygen to cells while extracting waste so the cells can grow and fuse together, forming the organ. Cells in a large 3D organ structure cannot maintain their metabolic functions without this ability, which is traditionally provided by blood vessels.

Working with his colleagues in Iowa, Dr. Ozbolat hopes to overcome the problem of thick tissue fabrication by bioprinting 'microfluidic channels' that can temporarily take on the function of a natural vascular network. Such channels will be 3D printed by two fluid dispensing nozzles, one of which will carry the required biomaterial, and the other a hardener to solidify it. At present a multiple-arm robot is being developed so that microfluidic channels can be bioprinted in tandem with the build-up of bio-ink tissue spheroids and bio-paper.

Recently I caught up with Dr. Ozbolat to ask about the progress of his work, and in particular his short- and longer-term goals. As he informed me, his short-term goal is 'to bioprint a pancreatic organ that is glucose sensitive' and which works in the lab. In the medium-term his hope is to transplant such a bioprinted organ into an animal and to successfully 'hook it up to its vascular system'. In the long-term, Dr Ozbolat wishes to develop the 'ultimate economical and feasible technology' that will allow stem cells to be used to bioprint a pancreatic organ that can be successfully transplanted anywhere inside the human body to regulate the glucose level of the blood.

As Dr. Ozbolat highlighted in his *Industrial Engineer* article, achieving his above goals will not be easy. As he stressed to me, challenges ahead include not just the vascular network problem that he is currently working to overcome, but additionally reducing cell damage during the bioprinting process and improving maturation times. And yet, like many other bioprinting researchers worldwide, Dr Ozbolat clearly remains convinced that one day bioprinting will result in a medical revolution.

SCAFFOLDS, TEETH & BONES

So far in this chapter I have focused on bioprinting research that is intent on the 3D output of layers of living tissue. There are, however, medical pioneers who are already accomplishing amazing things by 3D printing in non-living materials. I therefore want to side-step for a page or few to highlight how 3D printers are set to revolutionize medicine even when they are not directly outputting living cells.

Back in chapter 4 I explained how Bespoke Innovations are already using 3D printers to improve artificial limbs. Even more radically, a 60-year-old man from Essex in the United Kingdom was recently given a 3D printed silicon prosthetic to replace a section of his face. As reported by Richard Gray in *The Sunday Telegraph*, part of the left side of Eric Moger's face was removed during cancer surgery. A new, flexible 3D printed 'mask' was subsequently created for him by a dental surgeon called Andrew Dawood. This forms a seal at the top of Eric's mouth, so allowing him to once again eat and drink in a normal fashion. The mask is held in place by magnets so that it can be removed overnight.

Going beyond external prosthetics, some patients have already had 3D printed artefacts implanted inside their body. For example, in 2012 an 83-year-old woman in the UK was fitted with an artificial jaw that was laser-sintered in titanium. The elderly lady in question had been suffering from a bone infection called osteomyelitis which had destroyed much of her own jaw. Her new 3D printed jaw therefore provided her with a significant quality-of-life improvement.

As the above cases demonstrate, even today's 3D printing technologies have the potential to be used as part of a traditional medical armoury. Given that medical-grade thermoplastics (such as ABSi) already exist, it is also quite possible that fairly soon small prosthetic implants – like hernia meshes or even heart valves – may be 3D printed to patient specification outside or even inside the operating theatre.

An additional possibility is that future bioprinters will be used to manufacture custom scaffolds that will allow a patient to 'naturally' repair or regrow damaged body parts. In pursuit of this goal, several bioprinting research teams are already working to perfect the engineering of lattice-like scaffold structures. Not least, as I mentioned in the opening of this chapter, Anthony Atala's work at the Wake Forest

Institute for Regenerative Medicine started with the creation of artificial bladders built up in the lab by seeding scaffold molds with living cells. While these particular scaffolds were not 3D printed, already the idea of 3D printing similar support structures is now well beyond the drawing board.

For example, 3D printer manufacturer EnvisionTEC has worked with the Freiburg Materials Research Centre in Germany to produce its '3D-Bioplotter'. Like Organovo's NovoGen MMX, this builds up layers of tissue spheroids that are supported and protected during printout by layers of hydrogels. In addition, the EnvisonTEC Bioplotter can also output a number of biodegradable polymers and ceramics that may be used to support and help form artificial organs. Alternatively, the 3D-Bioplotter may be used solely to create scaffolds for implantation into patients.

A team under the leadership of Jeremy Mao at the Tissue Engineering and Regenerative Medicine Lab at Columbia University has already demonstrated the extraordinary possibilities. In one experiment, the team 3D printed an open 3D scaffold in the shape of an incisor. This featured tiny, interconnecting microchannels that were seeded with 'stem cell-recruiting substances'. As part of the experiment, the incisor scaffold was implanted into the jaw bone of a rat. Just nine weeks after implantation, this triggered the growth of fresh periodontal ligaments and newly formed alveolar bone. What this means is that, in the future, dentists may be able to implant 3D printed scaffolds into their patients that will stimulate their body to grow new teeth.

In a related research study, Mao and his team have also pioneered techniques that may allow patients to regrow new joints around bioprinted scaffolds. In this experiment 3D scans were taken of the hips of several mature rabbits. These were then used to bioprint 3D scaffolds upon which cartilage and bone could be regenerated.

Once printed, the scaffolds were infused with growth factors before being implanted into the rabbits in place of their own hip joints. As Mao's team reported in *The Lancet*, over a four-month period the rabbits all grew new and fully functional joints. Some of Mao's test subjects even began to walk and otherwise place weight on their new bone and cartilage only three or four weeks after surgery. In the future, the potential may therefore exist to use 3D printing to help those with joint problems to grow their own natural replacements, rather than being fitted with artificial knees or hips. In addition to the work being undertaken by Mao at Columbia University, research into the 3D printing of bone scaffolds is also being undertaken by Yuanyuan Li and a team at Shanghai University in China.

IN VIVO BIOPRINTING

As a third alternative to the printout of organs in the lab, or the creation of scaffolds, future bioprinters may add cells directly to the human body. Such a startling idea takes us right back to the work of pioneer Anthony Atala at the Wake Forest Institute for Regenerative Medicine. Here experiments have already begun to bioprint cells onto a patient *in vivo*. Specifically, working with a grant from the US Army, researchers at Wake Forest are trying to develop bioprinting techniques that could be used to treat burn victims as a surgical alternative to using skin grafts.

In preliminary experiments, a laser scanner has been used to produce 3D models of test injuries inflicted on mice. Data from these models has then been used to guide material jetting bioprinter heads that have sprayed layers of skin cells, a coagulant and collagen onto the rodent's wounds. Already the prototype *in vivo* bioprinter under test is fairly sophisticated, and able to determine just what needs to be deposited on which part of the wound and to what thickness.

Initial results have proved very promising, with the injuries on the mice treated with the bioprinter healing in just two or three weeks, compared to five or six weeks in a control group where the wounds were left to heal naturally. It has to be stressed that at present this research is in a very early, pre-clinical phase. Even so, the hope is that *in vivo* bioprinters will be used to treat human patients maybe a decade from now.

Already there is some evidence that the use of bioprinting to treat burn victims may result in fewer infections and less scarring than when applying a skin graft. In part this is because a major problem with skin graft burn treatment is obtaining enough tissue to cover and seal a wound. With appropriate technologies in place, the use of a 3D 'skin printer' could overcome this limitation, as enough cells could always be cultured from a patient biopsy and rapidly applied. A conceptual illustration of a future 3D skin printer appears in figure 7.3.

The development of *in vivo* bioprinting may one day not even be limited to printing new skin cells onto the outside of the body. At present, most forms of surgery create a wound in healthy flesh through which instruments and usually fingers are then inserted to perform a stitch, staple, graft or transplant repair. Following an operation, patients therefore have to heal both internally and at the wound site. But fast-forward a few decades, and it may be possible for robotic surgical arms tipped with bioprint heads to enter the body, repair damage, and even heal their point of entry on their way out. Patients would still need to rest and recuperate as bioprinted materials fully fused into cohesive living tissue. Even so, when treated in this manner, healthy patients could potentially recover from very major surgery in less than a week.

In an article in the January–February 2011 edition of *The Futurist*, bioprinting pioneer Vladimir Mironov imagined how *in vivo* bioprinting may actually work in practice. In a fictional future scenario, a football star injures his knee mid-season with severe cartilage damage, and undergoes immediate surgery. As Mironov continues the tale:

> At the start of the operation, four endoscopic devices are introduced into the star athlete's knee cavity. One has a miniature camera attached to it that enables the operating surgeon to see, the second provides laser technology, a third device eliminates tissue, and the fourth injects living stem cells isolated from the patient's fat tissue and suspended in hydrogel.

> The robot, controlled by a surgeon visually monitoring the procedure, removes the damaged cartilage using a tissue plasma evaporator. Next, the patient's own stem cells mixed with hydrogel are injected into the area and immediately polymerized by the laser beam. Finally, the endoscopic operating tools are removed and the injured skin is sprayed with a mixture of self-assembling skin cells suspended in hydrogel.

According to Mironov's prediction, such an operation could be completed in 20 minutes, with the patient walking out of the operating theatre and returning to the football field the next day. In time, the procedure could be used not just to mend damaged knees, but as a cure for arthritis and even to accomplish major surgery. After all, why bioprint new organs outside of the body (so inflicting major transplant surgery on a patient) if old organs can be removed and new ones 'fitted' one cell layer at a time?

If the above, well-informed scenarios where not enough, some twenty to thirty years from now *in vivo* bioprinting

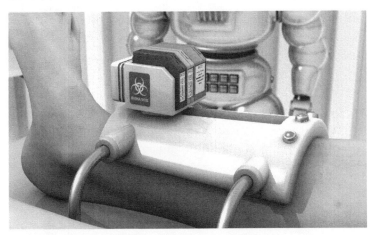

Figure 7.3: Concept Illustration of a 3D Skin Printer.
Image created by Christopher Barnatt, ExplainingTheFuture.com.

might be so safe and routine that it starts to be used cosmetically. As I argued in my book *25 Things You Need to Know About the Future*:

> A great many technological innovations that are created for one purpose end up being used for another. For example, modern plastic surgery techniques were developed to help rebuild the bodies and lives of burn victims and others who suffered horrific accidents. However, as we all know, plastic surgery is now performed far more commonly for cosmetic reasons than out of medical necessity. As and when [*in vivo*] bioprinting evolves into a routine and refined practice, its cosmetic application is similarly likely to skyrocket.
>
> A few decades hence it may become possible to use a bioprinter to radically, rapidly and fairly safely

transform the human body. Want bigger muscles without the exercise? Then why not visit your local bioprinting clinic and have them printed into your body that afternoon? Or fancy going skiing but worried about breaking your legs? Then why not have your bones replaced with new ones that feature carbon nanotube enforcements? These top-of-head scenarios may sound both fantastical and scary. Yet they may well be just the tip of a cosmetic bioprinting iceberg.

One day we may even see cosmetic bioprinters like the one I imagine in figure 7.4. Here a 'face printer' has been created that can remove unwanted layers of flesh, bone and other tissue and replace them with new bioprinted cells according to the patient's specification. Want to look like your favourite celebrity? Then just download a scan of their face from Thingiverse and have it applied in your local bioprinting bureau. Or fancy redesigning your nose on an iPad 27? No problem, by 2042 there could well be an app for that. Or simply worry about looking old? Well no problem, just get your face scanned when you are a teenager and have it 'reapplied' every five or ten years to achieve apparent perpetual youth.

OK, so these admittedly flippant scenarios may sound both ludicrous and utterly repugnant. Nevertheless, as and when *in vivo* bioprinting becomes a reality, so a machine like that shown in figure 7.4 may well be a technical possibility. Of course this does not mean that anybody would ever want to use it. Who, after all, would ever *choose* to have their face re-bioprinted? Let alone run the risk of such a procedure going wrong? In response I would simply note that every year millions of people *already* risk the considerable dangers of surgery purely to try and improve their looks.

Figure 7.4: Concept Illustration of a 3D Face Printer.
Image created by Christopher Barnatt, ExplainingTheFuture.com.

Vanity has always been an enormous business and is probably unlikely to shrink. Once the potential exists to have cosmetic face-replacement surgery, at least a few crazed individuals are therefore likely to sign up to have an application of the ultimate in living, designer make-up. Though once they have successfully undergone the procedure, we may well not know who they are.

A COMING OF AGE

While 3D printing has been used in industry since the 1980s, the science and practice of bioprinting is a 21st century development that is still fighting to emerge from the lab. This said, a professional bioprinting research community has now become very well established, with the specialist academic journal *Biofabrication* launched in 2009, and the International Society for Biofabrication (ISBF) founded in 2010. As Vladimir Mironov, Makoto Nakamura and Fabian Guillemot pronounced in their editorial in the second edition of *Biofabrication*, it is therefore already 'safe to state that bioprinting technology is coming of age'.

Perhaps reflecting the above, just like its 'traditional' 3D printing cousin, bioprinting is already attracting the attention of the DIY or 'maker' community. For example, over at instructables.com/id/DIY-BioPrinter it is now possible to download a pdf 'instructable' that will teach you how to convert a standard inkjet printer into a device that can print out cells. Granted, nobody is going to use this information to create new internal organs, to mend wounds, or to redesign their face anytime soon. Yet the fact that bioprinting is now both a hobbyist and professional pursuit does strongly suggest that it is here to stay. In the age of the Internet, the things that enthusiasts may potentially achieve in their basements and garages – and indeed on their kitchen tables – should also not be ignored.

The parallel development of new technologies by both amateurs and professionals is now becoming increasingly common, at least in the early phase. Technologies that evolve in both the professional and amateur spheres are also less likely to become entirely corporately owned, with a few individual makers or hackers fairly certain to keep at least a finger or two in the final pie. When it comes to the 3D Printing Revolution, I think it is also already very safe to suggest that the role of the individual 'amateur' is set to be increasingly important. Granted, the vast majority of those innovations that will allow 3D printing to enter the mainstream will come from corporate labs. But we should never forget that 3D printing is a technology that almost by definition is set to empower individuals by permitting new opportunities for personalized manufacturing anytime and anywhere.

Because 3D printing has the potential to place the means of production into the hands of most ordinary citizens, there are already those who believe that when the technology goes mainstream it will challenge capitalism itself. Personally I think that such a view is too extreme. Nevertheless, it is probably not over-the-top to suggest that a dawning 3D Printing Revolution is set to transform certain aspects of our lives, and not only in the field of medicine. The transformative potential of 3D printing therefore has to be the focus of our final chapter.

8

BRAVE NEW WORLD?

As I emerged from Old Street underground station it was a cold but dry January day. A few months back I had been in London to attend the UK's first major 3D printing event. But this time I had an appointment with environmental pressure group Friends of the Earth.

After a short, brisk walk I arrived at the Friends of the Earth headquarters and was soon being greeted by Mike Childs, their Head of Policy, Research and Science. Shortly thereafter I gave a lunchtime presentation that appeared to keep my audience engaged. I then sat down with Mike to discuss technological and environmental matters more generally.

As a YouTuber I happened to have a camera with me, and also happened to record an interview! In this Mike talked eloquently about a range of issues, and in particular made the following statement:

> I think one of the great things about some of the technologies that are being developed now – and 3D printing is a great example – is how they might actually disrupt an economic system that has developed over the last 20 years to be a globalized system with very few actors . . . [Technologies like 3D

printing] could be a real disruptive influence that may lead to more localization, more local production, and less dominance of the major multinationals.

Like Mike I believe that 3D printing will challenge many conventional norms, and that in particular it may help us to build more local and more sustainable economies. Mike and I are also far from alone in believing in 3D printing's transformative potential. For example, when I interviewed Mark Fleming – the founder of the website 3Dprinter.net – he made the following observation:

> 3D printing destroys the inefficient, 20th century manufacturing model and replaces it with a new paradigm that brings a reduction in design-to-manufacturing time, virtually eliminates storage and transportation costs, reduces resource consumption, allows us to make things that were not possible before, and democratizes the materialization of ideas so literally everyone can create. 3D printing will do to manufacturing what the Internet has done to communication.

FANTASY FUTURES

So far in this book I have looked at the grassroots practicalities of 3D printing, as well as the activities of its industrial and consumer pioneers. In doing so I have tried to look to the future by pointing to cutting edge things that are possible and happening right now. This approach has I hope kept things grounded, with science fiction very much left on the back burner. Though now, in this final chapter, it is time to open things up as I explore 3D printing's broader implications.

By 2030 you could be waking up in a house 3D printed out of bonded sand or sprayed concrete. Look to the right, and you may be greeted by a smile on your spouse's bio-printed face. Or roll-over to the left, and you could watch as the food printer on your bedside table fabricates hot sausages and bacon one thin layer at a time.

Overnight, your wardrobe 3D printer may have ground up an old pair of shoes, and then used the reclaimed synthetic leather to manufacture some new footwear in the latest fashion. Meanwhile, out in the garden, a hoard of synthetic bacteria could be fermenting your family's excrement from the previous week into some brand-spanking-new PLA filament. This could then be used by your eight-year-old daughter to 3D print the new Barbie doll that she customized on the smartphone that you had fabricated for her last birthday.

Later that day you could visit a store that has no stock whatsoever, but which can – in less than an hour – industrially fabricate any product that has ever existed. Of course, you would not be expected to wait for the manufacture-on-demand of your desired goods, as a 3D printed humanoid robot would bring them to your home on its eco-friendly 3D printed bicycle.

While waiting at home for your purchases to arrive, you may well reflect on what life was like in the heyday of globalization when things travelled far more than people. In those seemingly distant days you and your friends worked in a factory making vehicles that are now churned out on garage forecourts by machines that also wash the cars they manufacture. But no matter, you will soon be flying in a clear, plastic, 3D printed airliner to see your brother who is about to be fitted with bioprinted gills so that he can live underwater while he supervises the 3D re-printing of the Great Barrier Reef.

OK. I could go on. But I think you get the point. If some of the most 'optimistic' pundits are right, fairly soon 3D printers will work much like the replicators on *Star Trek: The Next Generation*, and all industries will be transformed by unlimited new manufacturing possibilities. Indeed, there are now those who claim that, in little more than a decade, 3D printing will have advanced so significantly that nothing will be manufactured by traditional means, personal recycling will be commonplace, medicine will have been transformed, and almost all human labour will be a service activity.

Not least given my work as a futurist, I totally get where people are coming from when they claim that 3D printing will sooner or later transform virtually all aspects of our lives and our economy. In fact, if developments in 3D printing mirror recent advancements in computing, ought we really to expect anything less?

As I argued way back in the *Preface*, it is very important to recognise today's 3D printers as no more than a stepping stone to tomorrow's far more sophisticated machines. Nevertheless, we need to be realistic. 3D printing is going to be revolutionary. But just as the majority of today's Internet Age work and leisure activities would be familiar to somebody from the 1970s, so I greatly suspect that ten, twenty or even fifty years from now, many traditional manufacturing processes will still be being practised just as they are today.

3D printing is going to alter how some things are made, and how a great many traditional manufacturing processes are tooled-up. This said, just as computing devices have not made pens, pencils, paper and all manner of traditional 'information media' entirely redundant, so 3D printing is not going to replace all forms of traditional manufacturing. 3D printing will be 'revolutionary' even if it changes how perhaps 20 per cent of things are manufactured, transported and stored. The key thing for us to try and foresee is therefore just which industrial activities 3D printing is most likely to 'revolutionize', as well as those which are more probable to remain untouched.

BUILDING A BETTER FUTURE?

To try and gain a realistic perspective, let me work more slowly through the range of predictions contained in my above 'fantasy futures' scenario. My fictional picture of tomorrow began with the suggestion of 3D printed buildings, and here I would contend that, by 2030, the construction industry really is going to have witnessed a certain degree of 3D-printing-related change.

As reported in March 2013 by Ari Honka on 3Dprintingindustry.com, Dutch designers DUS Architects are already planning to 3D print a full-size house on the bank of the Buiksloter canal in northern Amsterdam. They are going to do this using their experimental KamerMaker (or 'room maker') 3D printer. This resides in a shipping container, and will output the canal house in sections as large as 2.2 x 2.2 x 3.47 m (7.2 x 7.2 x 11.4 feet). The hope is to complete the facade and first room of the building by the end of 2013.

While the KamerMaker is impressive, at present it only 3D prints in rigid plastic. Because of this, it is not going to change how most future buildings are made. Even so, as Thomas Frey recently argued in his blog for *The Futurist*, 3D printing will still probably result in the 'biggest construction boom in all history'.

Alongside the KamerMaker, and as we saw in chapter 4, 3D printers that extrude cement or spray a binder onto sand have already demonstrated the potential to release architects from the constraints of currently buildable structures. The 3D Printing Revolution is therefore set to allow a far more fluid use of curves in building construction. Material savings and improved insulation are also major possibilities, as cavities will be able to be printed into walls, floors, roofs and other building components. The headaches involved in transporting large pre-made parts to building sites are also likely to diminish, as massive, complex geometries will be able to be fabricated *in situ*.

So, by 2030, are you really likely to wake up in an entirely 3D printed building? The answer is probably not, unless you are foolish or unfortunate enough to have taken to sleeping in the latest gazebos or bus shelters. Nevertheless, what is quite possible is that, in addition to small 3D printed structures, some of our most complex new buildings will feature at least a few 3D printed sections.

REPRINTING OURSELVES

Moving on to the next part of my 2030 scenario, without a crystal ball it is impossible to predict whether or not many years hence you will wake up next to a smiling spouse. But if you do, the chances are than in 2030 their face will still be made of the same flesh that they were born with. However, their body – or your own come to that – could quite possibly contain one or two bioprinted parts. Not least, it is extremely likely that one or both of you will have a bioprinted crown or tooth.

As the last chapter hopefully made clear, bioprinting is a technology that looks set to transform not just dentistry, but certain surgical practices. For foolhardy individuals with the money, by 2040 or 2050 cosmetic face printing and body-reforming is likely to be on the cards. Yet well before this occurs, bioprinted arterial grafts, skin grafts, heart valves and probably kidneys will become a reality. Indeed, based on my communications with those conducting today's bioprinting research, the development of bioprinted kidneys by 2030 (and perhaps by 2025) is a realistic proposition. Such 'artificial' organs will probably not look or function exactly like a natural human kidney or duplicate all of its features. Yet for thankful patients this will not matter provided that their new, bioprinted kidneys are capable of surviving in their body and cleaning waste products from their blood.

If, by 2030, you have suffered an injury or are getting on in years, you may well also have a new bone or some joint cartilage that was formed 'naturally' around a bioprinted scaffold. At present the potential implantation of bioprinted meshes to allow the body to accomplish its own major repairs really does look very promising. The routine use of bioprinters to help heal failed hips and knees is therefore quite likely sometime next decade.

More broadly, given that health and beauty are the largest industry in the world, I would suggest that bioprinting has a very promising future. A lot of investment will be needed to get the technology out of the lab and into our bodies if we are ever to bioprint major organs or to repair patients with internal bioprinting hardware. Yet healthcare expenditures globally are already massive and rising. This is, after all, why Organovo has managed to find the funding to float on the stock market ahead of so many 'traditional' 3D printer manufacturers.

The fact that the population is ageing also needs to be taken into account. OK, so not all older people will have the money to afford bioprinted medical prosthesis. But some will be rich enough to buy them, with many older people likely to sacrifice greatly to try and increase their quality of life. Governments are also likely to want to invest in bioprinting if it can help to keep the poorer old in a productive and healthy state for as long as possible. Active octogenarians with bioprinted body parts will after all be far less of a burden on the state than those who have to spend their later years languishing in hospitals and nursing homes.

FOOD GLORIOUS FOOD

Throughout this book the subject of food printing has largely been noticeable by its absence. I have made a couple of references to the 3D printing of customized chocolates or cake decorations, and am certain that this kind of thing will happen in the future not least because it is already happening today. I am, however, far from convinced that a food printer like that included on the bedside table in my 2030 fantasy future will ever exist. This also puts me at odds with some highly respected 3D printing advocates who believe that soon personal fabricators will routinely output nutritionally balanced meals. For example, as Hod Lipson argues in his book *Fabricated*, 'the new personal chef will be a 3D printer in your kitchen, one that's hooked up to the Internet to await text messages or e-mail instructions about your next meal'.

The above prediction I believe to be fundamentally flawed. And to explain why, we simply have to consider the various ways in which food could technically be created in layers using 3D printing hardware.

Firstly, food printers may simply extrude existing, premixed foodstuffs – such as cake frosting, soft cheese or melted chocolate – that will then readily set to create custom products. Commercial chocolate printers that can do just this, such as the Choc Creator V1 from Choc Edge, are already on the market for a few thousand dollars. It is therefore very likely that some canny entrepreneurs will develop successful businesses that produce customized Easter eggs, Valentine's Day chocolates or birthday cake decorations. This kind of food printing is not going to change the world. Even so, we can be pretty certain that some people will on special occasions pay $30 or more for $3 of chocolate, frosting or cheese that has been custom 3D printed.

Secondly, food printers may extrude an uncooked food substance that then needs to be baked. Hod Lipson, for example, has already demonstrated a Fab@Home printer outputting cookie dough that was then placed in an oven. More sophisticated food printers may perhaps even be loaded with multiple ingredients that get mixed in controlled combination in their print heads. This could allow a food printer to put a recipe together. Once again, a very few people may choose to do this. But I cannot help thinking that those who like to cook will prefer to stick to traditional culinary methods. Meanwhile non-chefs will probably not want the hassle of loading a food printer with a range of ingredients (and spending lots of time cleaning it out afterwards), when they can pick up a McDonalds on the way home, order a takeaway on their smartphone, or expend less effort transferring a ready meal from a freezer to a microwave.

We also need to remember that we are fast approaching a future in which, due to oil and other resource shortages, we will not always be able to favour a machine over human labour. The idea that we will soon use 3D printers to make mainstream food preparation even more energy and resource intensive is therefore farcical.

We additionally need to bear in mind the supposed problems that all kinds of 3D printers may be trying to solve. Today, most citizens do not have the ability or the tools to craft spare parts for their washing machine, lawn mower or bicycle. A domestic 3D printer that may allow them to make such parts may therefore have value in *some* homes. In stark comparison, most people can prepare food, learn to prepare food, buy pre-prepared food, eat out, or become friends with a chef. I therefore think that the vast majority of the population will stick with food sourced from shops and restaurants, or which they or others can make cheaper and probably better than a food printer. Yes, a few gadget freaks will love the idea of spending the weekend printing out a slice of bread. But a mainstream technology in the waiting? Give me a break.

Finally we get to the notion of future food printers that will output synthetic meat. This is, I freely admit, a clear technical possibility. After all, by the time we can bioprint a living, functional human kidney, we will certainly be able to output a non-functional and entirely dead steak, sausage or slice of bacon. But again, whether this will be a sensible or economically practical idea is another matter entirely.

Just as the bioprinting of human tissue has to start with the culturing of human cells, so the potential future 3D printing of synthetic meat would initially require the growth of animal cells. These may perhaps be cultured *in vitro* using cells obtained from a host animal. Alternatively, synthetic bacteria may one day be able to turn plants or algae into fresh meat cells. That is, after all, what a cow, pig or sheep does, and the bacteria will not have to waste time mucking about with bones, eyes, brains, mooing, and an excessive flatulence of greenhouse gasses.

So, let us suppose that we get really good at growing 'real' or 'artificial' animal cells for table. What will we then do with these cells? Well, we could just lump them together to create synthetic meat products and get on with cooking and eating them. Or, we could spray layer-upon layer of individual meat cells – or extrude vast quantities of tiny biomeat spheroids – in order to create pretty slabs of customized meat using future 3D food printers.

Economics alone ought to inform us that there is no competition here. People will have to be very rich indeed to want to increase the cost of synthetic meat by bioprinting it out, as the process would basically involve taking a culture of synthetic material, breaking it down into very tiny parts, and then sticking it back together again.

Due to the above, making any connection between future bioprinting and potential future meat printing is grossly naïve. A human kidney bioprinted in the lab, or better still straight into a patient's abdomen, would be good value for both the patient and society at large even if it cost many thousands of dollars. In comparison, a steak, sausage or meat pie about the size of a human kidney would not be a remotely cost effective proposition if it cost more than a few dollars. Given that it is exceedingly unlikely that growing cells and then bioprinting them out is ever going to be mastered at this price point, I feel very safe in my dismissal of bioprinted meat as quite literal future pie in the sky.

MAKING OUR OWN STUFF

Right, so what about the idea that by 2030 we will be routinely 3D printing out our own custom products? Not to mention grinding up old shoes to make new ones, or turning human waste into a bioplastic that our kids then 3D print into toys? Well, at least in comparison to food printing, these propositions are far more realistic. Home devices – such as Tyler McNaney's Filabot – that can turn plastic waste into fresh 3D printing supplies are likely to be widely available well before the end of this decade, let alone by 2030. The synthetic biotech that will allow human or animal waste to be cheaply and locally fermented into bioplastics, biofuels or bioacrylics also has the potential to go mass-market by 2020. This means that the notion of domestically 3D printing plastic things from recycled or otherwise home-sourced materials is based on pretty solid current fact.

As we saw in chapter 5, consumer thermoplastic extrusion 3D printers are becoming more and more widely available. Within a decade they will probably also be a cheap and reliable technology that will allow the domestic, one-click fabrication of many useful objects in a range of existing and new plastic materials. Such domestic 3D printers will absolutely not allow individual citizens to fabricate complex things like smartphones or other electronic items. But home-printed toys, tableware, ornaments, brackets, shoes, containers, fashion accessories and many other items are a distinct medium-term possibility.

The above point noted, it must be understood that anything we 3D print at home will be somewhat different to most of the products that clutter our houses and apartments today. Just as the possessions owned by most people were very different before and after the first Industrial Revolution, so we ought not to expect the new production technology of the 3D Printing Revolution to make things that are exactly like those churned out by today's highly centralized industrial plant. Building objects in layers, and traditional casting or molding, are very different processes that will never produce exactly the same results. If you want a 3D printed plastic object that feels like it was injection molded you will I am afraid be waiting a very long time indeed.

As I argued back in chapter 6, in a decade or so the whole context of our lives will have started to shift – and not due to 3D printing, but because of an increase in the price and a decrease in the availability of petroleum and other key natural resources. In turn, this will drive a new wave of localization and a return to some level of domestic manufacture. It is also in this context that 3D printing will become a revolutionary technology. If you have an eight year old daughter in 2030, she will not 3D print a new Barbie doll on a home 3D printer as an alternative to a toy mass produced in China. Rather, a doll 3D printed at home (or at a local bureau) will for most families be the only option.

While the Maker Movement is growing, we really have not seen anything yet. Sometime between 2020 and 2030 I strongly suspect that the home-spun manufacture of a reasonable proportion of our possessions will once again start to become the norm. This absolutely does not mean that everything we own will be home-printed, home-sewn, home-repaired or home-grown. But no longer will a scarf knitted by Grandma, or a birthday card made by a child, be unusual because it did not come out of a very distant industrial plant.

What all of this means is that the 3D Printing Revolution will – at least on the domestic level – be as much about a new means of ownership as a new means of manufacture. By 2030 I am quite certain that we will not just buy less, but that most of us will have a significant quantity of either home-made or very-locally-made possessions. This was after all the norm until the beginning of the last Industrial Revolution. In a near-future world in which resource and energy scarcity again makes mother the necessity of invention, 3D printing may therefore greatly increase our quality of life by allowing us to own a far wider range of goods than would otherwise be possible.

MANUFACTURE ON DEMAND

While by 2030 home-produced items may be fairly common, most if fewer things are still likely to be commercially manufactured. As I have already suggested, many of these products will still be made using existing processes like casting and injection molding. This is simply because, when it comes to producing large quantities of standardized goods, current production methods are not just very good indeed, but also make a great deal of sense.

A factory that currently injection molds several million identical biro casings every year would be insane to even consider producing such low-cost, high-volume items using a 3D printer. Granted, switching to molds created using direct metal laser sintering (DMLS) would be a great idea when design changes require re-tooling. However, where transportation to an end customer remains a realistic proposition, it will usually be more economic to inject plastic into a mold rather than to extrude it one thin layer at a time.

But, I hear some 3D printing advocates cry, surely in time 3D printing will become cost competitive with all forms of injection molding? After all, the cost of information technology has continued to fall by orders of magnitude. So surely we just have to wait for the same to occur with 3D printing?

Unfortunately, the above common argument is sadly flawed, as digital information processing and physical manufacture are two very different kinds of activity. Over the past few decades, the processing and communication of digital information may well have speeded up exponentially. But information exchange does not have to deal with physical realities like viscosity and friction that will always limit the speed of physical production processes including 3D printing. Certainly 3D printing is going to get a lot faster and cheaper. Even so, we ought to expect its direct manufacturing application to be limited to the production of relatively high value, low-run, rare or customized products and components.

Returning to my 2030 scenario, it is subsequently unlikely that any store two decades hence will fabricate everything on demand (unless, of course, it is a local 3D printing bureau). Rather, I would expect in-store 3D manufacture to be limited mainly to the production of custom products, and in particular spare parts. A few decades out, mass consumerism is likely to have been replaced with a new culture that of necessity champions repair over replacement. By 2030, when we visit a store to get something 3D printed, it will therefore be just as likely to be a new component for a product we already own, rather than a completely new item.

Turning to vehicle production, in my 2030 scenario I mused that automobiles may one day be fabricated on garage forecourts. While 3D printing entire vehicles is unlikely, the idea of fabricating new body panels at a garage is a technical near-future possibility, and especially so if we start to drive composite or plastic vehicles. As I reported in chapter 4, already the majority of a new, low-energy vehicle called the Urbee has been 3D printed. To expect garages to own automotive 3D printers is therefore not that unrealistic a proposition. Cars are, after all, expensive to store and to ship. Certain components – like engines, drive shafts, tyres and electronics – could by 2030 therefore be delivered to local dealerships who would 3D print less sophisticated components and perform final assembly. This is especially likely if we transition en-masse to electric vehicles, as these will require the use of lightweight materials and will typically be constructed from fewer components.

Finally in my fantasy future scenario, I hinted at a 3D printed humanoid robot making deliveries on a 3D printed bicycle, not to mention a 3D printed aircraft, and a person being fitted with bioprinted gills to enable them to work underwater 3D re-printing the Great Barrier Reef. While all of these were fanciful suggestions, none are in fact entirely outlandish. For a start a 3D printed bicycle – the 'Airbike' – has already been produced by the European Aerospace and Defence Group (EADS). This was laser sintered in white nylon, has the same strength as a metal equivalent, but is 65 per cent lighter. To quote a 2011 article from *Engadget*, 'it also looks rather decent'.

While 3D printing a humanoid robot will be somewhat harder than fabricating it a bicycle, functional humanoid robots are likely to be walking among us sometime in the 2030s. They are also very likely to have 3D printed components, as future androids are extremely probable to be highly expensive and at least semi-customized. Robots with 3D printed parts would also be the easiest to repair, and may even have integrated 3D printers to facilitate self-repair. No intelligent creature has ever successfully evolved without at least some level of self-repair capability. We should therefore expect 3D printing and robot evolution to go hand in material-extruded hand.

And 3D printed airliners? Well I would place a safe bet that planes with 3D printed wings and fuselage sections will be safely flying people around by 2030. Already the aviation industry is runways ahead of most others in its development of the technology. EADS did not, after all, 3D print a plastic bicycle because it wanted to enter the Tour de France.

So this leaves us with the bizarre notion of a person being fitted with bioprinted gills to help them work underwater in the 3D re-printing of the Great Barrier Reef. This just has to be utter garbage, does it not? Well, with parallel developments in genetic medicine and bioprinting, the gills concept to enable a person to breathe underwater may just work. Though even if it never happens (and divers for some reason decide to stick with traditional scuba gear), the 3D re-printing of damaged coral reefs is a very realistic possibility. In fact, an Australian company called Sustainable Oceans International (SOI) is already working with the Arabian Gulf's leading artificial reef construction company – Reef Arabia – to deploy the first 3D printed reef off the northern coast of Bahrain. OK, so before we get to the next section, you may want to go and lie down for a few minutes.

THE INEVITABLE DOWNSIDE

While manufacture-on-demand and food printing may not prove as widespread or even as possible as some currently believe, 3D printing is set to revolutionize significant areas of personal and industrial activity in very positive ways. This said, there will inevitably be a few major downsides for us to contend with. No new technology has ever managed to invade our lives without wreaking a little havoc, and 3D printing will be no different.

For example, cosmetic bioprinting could have potentially unintended consequences if people can use future 'face printers' to constantly 'roll-back' their appearance in pursuit of perpetual youth. Or as YouTube user 'Nickuncle' commented after watching the bioprinting video in which I demonstrate a future face printer in action:

> I just thought about the idea of teenagers re-applying their faces over and over. I mean, you'll go up to some total hottie, maybe be a little forward, be like 'damn girl, you're looking fine'. And she'll turn around and say, 'why thank you young man. These ol' bones ah mine have been holdin' in for 87 years now'.

Far more seriously, there are very real concerns that 3D printing will allow the personal fabrication of items that society may not want everybody to own. Most obviously, personal 3D printers could be used to duplicate keys or to fabricate all kinds of weapons or parts thereof. Indeed, as the YouTube user 'Ilovewinter' commented after watching another of my 3D printing videos:

> What I really like is the brand new application to allow anyone anywhere to print a firearm, or parts to a firearm. Most pistols are composite, and aside from the barrel that can be made quickly on CNC, the rest can be produced from a 3D printer, and parts purchased at any hardware store. I even hear it is even possible to make a single fire all plastic gun :) Nonetheless it will help us Americans hold on to

ours :) Since we can now print magazines with no trace as to when they were made.

To many people's alarm, the claims stated in the above comment are absolutely true. Already a 'wiki weapon project' called Defence Distributed has 3D printed entire sections of an AR-15 automatic rifle, and has made the digital blueprints freely available online. Defence Distributed also has plans to create open source designs for an entirely 3D printed firearm.

Hardly surprisingly, the future manufacture of plastic firearms on any desktop is causing concern in many quarters. Not only could such 3D printed guns get into the wrong hands, but they would be undetectable with a metal detector (although an X-ray scan would pick them out).

Aware of the issue, firms in the 3D printing industry are starting to take action. For example, in September 2012 Stratasys took back a uPrint SE 3D printer that it had leased to Corey Wilson – the creator of Defence Distributed – on the basis that he did 'not have a federal firearms manufacturers license'. The 3D object exchange website Thingiverse also has a clause in its Terms of Use that bans users from uploading anything that 'promotes illegal activities or contributes to the creation of weapons'. Though unfortunately, this has not stopped the site hosting designs for keys to high-security handcuffs, as well as realistic toy guns.

THE END OF INTELLECTUAL PROPERTY?

The exchange of 3D objects on websites like Thingiverse additionally raises the broader question of how intellectual property may be controlled as the 3D Printing Revolution takes hold. When I started planning this book I felt somewhat compelled to include a whole chapter on patents and copyright. Though as you will by now have noticed, such a chapter never materialized. Largely this was because I was not quite sure what I was expected to write about in such depth. Will 3D printing allow people to make copies of some physical things in a similar fashion to today's digital piracy of music and video? Yes, absolutely. So there were are. And while many manufacturers and lawyers will work hard to prevent this from happening, they are most likely to labour in vain.

Protecting intellectual property rights is in future going to prove increasingly difficult. While at present creating digital files that allow an existing, commercial product to be reproduced remains a fairly difficult and cumbersome activity, at least in some instances this will not remain the case for very long. In fact, in March 2013, MakerBot Industries demonstrated an early prototype of its forthcoming 'Digitizer Desktop 3D Scanner'. This is described as offering 'a quick and easy way to turn the things in your world into 3D designs you can share and print'. As Bre Pettis, the CEO of MakerBot, enthused:

> We are super excited to announce . . . that we are developing the MakerBot Digitizer Desktop 3D Scanner. It's a natural progression for us to create a product that makes 3D printing even easier. With the MakerBot Digitizer Desktop 3D Scanner, now everyone will be able to scan a physical item, digitize it, and print it in 3D – with little or no design experience.

The above may not have been heralded as such a marvellous development by the producer of the garden gnome that was demonstrated being 3D scanned and replicated on a MakerBot 3D printer. In fact, the designer of any solid object – or any object made from relatively few plastic, ceramic or even metal parts – may be rather disgruntled when domestic 3D scanners and 3D printers become widely available. We may be centuries away from true 'replicator' devices that could scan a smartphone, television or other complex item and print out a copy. But if a friend of yours has a particularly interesting plastic coat hanger, pair of flip-flops, bicycle helmet, lunchbox or figurine, then within a few years the means will be available for you to duplicate it fairly easily – or to find a digital copy of it already waiting online for free download.

As somebody who earns part of their living authoring books and making videos, I am absolutely not on the side of those who believe that stealing other people's intellectual property is an ethical or acceptable proposition. But I also think that the writing is now on the wall for designers of certain types of things. When asked in an interview how anybody can now protect their intellectual property, Janne Kyttanen – the 3D printing pioneer who founded Freedom of Creation – simply replied 'I don't believe in IP, trademarks, patents nor copyright'.

The above attitude is I fear becoming far more prominent, and is likely to continue to spread. Just as the purchasers of blank audio cassettes and video tapes in the 1980s and 1990s questioned what people *thought* they would use them for, so purchasers of personal 3D printers may soon be wondering *why* anybody is surprised that they are using them to duplicate things.

The potential illegal copying of physical objects – or 'physibles', as the Pirate Bay website calls them – is inevitably now attracting the attention of some in the legal profession, as well as a few wily inventors. Most notably, in October 2012 the US Patent Office issued a patent to an organization called The Invention Science Fund for a 'method for secure manufacturing to control object production rights'. In effect, this is a patent for a digital rights management (DRM) system for physical objects that would prevent a 3D printer from fabricating something that its owner did not have the right to fabricate.

In recent years DRM systems have had some success in curtailing the piracy of digital content such as music or videos. Nevertheless, it is exceptionally difficult to understand how any form of DRM will be able to prevent copies of objects being made. Not least, open source 3D printers are already a reality. So unless all open source designers and 3D printer builders choose to incorporate a globally implemented DRM system into their home-made hardware, the cat is already well and truly out of the bag.

3D printer DRM systems are also likely to fail due to the spread of open design. As makers and fabbers around the planet already highlight, in the near future people are likely not just to be digitally replicating commercial goods, but also altering them. In turn this will make it very difficult to argue just what is and what is not a copy of another object, and hence whose intellectual property may or may not have been stolen.

It is also the case that, while most people who make a copy of a movie or music track want the copy to exactly replicate the original, this same condition is a lot less likely to hold true when it comes to the future copying and sharing of physical stuff. Granted, some people will want certain designer goods or artworks to be identical to those they are seeking to duplicate. But in most instances it will be function rather than exact form that will matter.

As the previous few pages have hopefully highlighted, the 3D Printing Revolution is going to raise all kinds of design, patent and intellectual property issues. Quite what should or even can be done about this is currently very difficult to fathom. Though if you do want to know more, an attorney called Michael Weinberg has written some very detailed articles on the subject. The latest was published in January 2013, and is called *What's the Deal with Copyright and 3D Printing?* Mr Weinbeg's work can be read online or downloaded from publicknowledge.org/Copyright-3DPrinting. Though to my mind, the fact that this document is available for free says a great deal!

BROADER CONCERNS

In addition to intellectual property issues and the fabrication of undesirable things, the 3D Printing Revolution may potentially raise even wider concerns. One of these is health and safety, as objects produced at home or in a 3D printing bureau may potentially not be as safe as those mass-manufactured in a factory and subject to rigorous checks. Even a simple item like a mug could prove dangerous if the handle came away when it was full of a boiling beverage. 3D printing new parts to fix domestic appliances could also prove highly unsafe if they proved structurally unfit for purpose, and yet this is not necessarily the first thing that a domestic maker may take into account. Quite how this matter will in the future be accounted for is again unclear. I therefore suspect that we will hear far more about liability issues arising from faulty and dangerous 3D printed goods in the relatively near future.

A final major concern relates to the potential impact of the 3D Printing Revolution on employment. Today, almost everything we own is made in a factory at least in part by a fellow human being who is financially rewarded for their labours. But if domestic and local print-on-demand become common, what then? Will 3D printing prove the final nail in the coffin that forces many struggling businesses under and puts millions of out of work? And if so, is 3D printing something that most people should resist rather than welcome?

My first response to the above common worry is that, for a very, very long time to come, domestic fabrication and local manufacture-on-demand are going to be limited to high-value, customized objects and the production of spare parts. As I stated at the start of this chapter, 3D printing will be a revolutionary technology even if it 'only' alters how 20 per cent of things are manufactured, and that will leave 80 per cent of manufacturing practice and employment untouched. This is not to say that 3D printing will not cause jobs to be lost in some companies, sectors and nations. But, as the 3D printing industry flourishes, it will also create new employment. As every technology-led revolution up until the last one of the Internet ought to remind us, industrial transition only really occurs when people start doing new things in new ways, and those new things have typically been good for economic prosperity. I therefore suspect that 3D printing will prove far more of a springboard for industrial rejuvenation and economic recovery than a catalyst for unemployment.

We must also again remember that the 3D Printing Revolution will arrive in a very specific environmental and economic context. Many now claim that 3D printing will result in the 'repatriation' of jobs from China, India and other developing nations to the more stagnant economies of Europe and the United States. I have no doubt that over the next two decades such a migration of manufacturing employment will occur, and that 3D printing will play its part in allowing it to happen. Even so, I also believe that the decline of globalized industrial production and the rise of localization will be driven almost entirely by looming oil and resource shortages.

If, in two decades time, there is still cheap oil and a cheap overseas labour force to be exploited, then I suspect that most Western citizens and companies will still be taking advantage of them to produce most of our goods. This said, I simply do not believe that either cheap oil or (relatively) cheap overseas labour will actually exist in any quantity twenty years from now. As I argued many pages back, in the relatively near future we will 3D print some things not because it is the best manufacturing option, but because it will be the only viable means of obtaining them.

THE NEXT REVOLUTION?

Back in the 1980s and 1990s, many personal computing and Internet pioneers fiercely proclaimed that their new technologies would change the world. In contrast today, most of those who most strongly contend that 3D printing will utterly transform traditional manufacturing are not actually in the 3D printing business. This is not to suggest that today's 3D printer makers and digital manufacturing pioneers do not see great potential. Nevertheless, their future visions are usually far more grounded and realistic. In fact, some of today's most successful and innovative 3D printing pioneers even question the use of the 'revolution' label. For example, when I asked Miranda Bastijns, the Director of i.materialise and .MGX, if we really are about to witness a '3D Printing Revolution', she replied as follows:

> Revolution is a strong word. There are many that say the revolution will begin when the 'killer app' is found. However, instead of a single technological breakthrough that will transform this industry, there will be a steady series of advances in technology which will take place. There will be a multitude of smaller breakthroughs and the transition from a niche technology to a mainstream technology will happen steadily over time. Therefore, although we may look back in 15 years and realize that the tech-

nology has revolutionized how we live our lives, we may not notice it so clearly while it happens – much like people have slowly adapted to the Internet and mobile phones only to be shocked when they take a step back and see how far we have come over the last 15 years.

In this chapter I have tried to bring this book to a close with a realistic assessment of what the 3D Printing Revolution may actually be like. Like Miranda I believe that we will see an amalgamation of incremental change that will, in time, alter how many but by no means most things are made. I also think that many, many people really do not appreciate the potential significance of small changes in traditional manufacturing methods. In part this is because most European countries and the United States have ceased to be manufacturing nations. The consequences of being able to 3D print a functional prototype, a sand cast, or a few custom components for an otherwise traditionally-produced product, are therefore really not understood in many boardrooms. Nor are they appreciated in most business schools where it has been forgotten that 'business' is actually about making and delivering products and services, rather than devising 'strategies', practising 'human resource management' or running marketing campaigns.

While during the Internet Revolution many of us learnt entirely new things, the 3D Printing Revolution will be more of a period in which we remember and return to old ways. Human beings rose to planetary dominance due to our unique ability to reshape the physical world in line with our imagination. Collectively we are still pretty good at this. But in the decades ahead we will need to re-learn how to achieve great things in a more local and more resource-efficient manner. In part this will involve many citizens producing a little of their own stuff, or else talking nicely to friends and family members who can. Given that 3D printing will empower those who like to make things, it is subsequently set to play an important role in our gradual transition to a more sustainable mode of living.

Whatever happens, fairly soon 3D printing is going to be something that most people know about. While writing this last chapter I received an invitation to the opening of iMakr, London's first 3D printer store. Five or so years from now, such stores will exist in all cities, 3D printing bureaus will be even more common, and web services that allow anybody to upload and 3D print will be pretty much ubiquitous. Meanwhile, in studios and factories all over the world, 3D printers will be working away, layer-by-layer, assisting traditional design and manufacturing processes and allowing new production methods to evolve. Doctors will also be learning to bioprint regenerative scaffolds and transplantable human tissues, while children will be returning from school to impress proud parents with their latest 3D printed creations.

Ten years from now the 3D Printing Revolution will be just picking up speed. Yet even by that time it will probably be old news, with the revolution's true pioneers long since crowned, and mainstream journalistic attention seriously starting to drift. If you really want to be part of the 3D Printing Revolution you therefore need to act sooner rather than later. Never in history have the opportunities been so great for so many people to start designing and manufacturing things in new ways. If you are a potential pioneer in waiting, I therefore hope that the end of this book is actually a beginning. The future is always forged by those who are prepared to act rather than just think. So if you are up for the challenge, it is now time to 3D print.

GLOSSARY

3D printing is a technology and an industry already steeped in its own terminology. To help get you up to speed with this new lexicon, below is a glossary of key terms and abbreviations. Also included are the names of some organizations and printer models that frequently pop-up in discussion.

2PP
See two-photon polymerization.

3D PRINTING
Most people now use the term '3D printing' to refer to any technology that creates a solid object from computer data by building it up in a great many very thin layers. However, some engineers and hardware purists argue that '3D printing' (3DP) refers only to devices that additively manufacture objects using a binder jetting technology that sprays an adhesive onto successive layers of powder.

3D SAND CASTING
3D sand casting is a process that produces molds into which molten metal can be directly poured to produce final objects. The technology works either by jetting a foundry-grade resin onto successive layers of a specially engineered sand, or else fusing layers of sand together via selective laser sintering (SLS).

3D SYSTEMS

3D Systems Corporation is one of the largest manufacturers of 3D printers in the world. The company was formed by Charles Hull, who invented stereolithography and the first 3D printer in 1984. 3D Systems has grown very rapidly via acquisition, and provides 3D printers and 3D printing services for a broad range of applications spanning industrial clients to end consumers.

3DP

See 3D printing

ABS

See acrylonitrile butadiene styrene.

ACRYLONITRILE BUTADIENE STYRENE

Acrylonitrile butadiene styrene (ABS) is a common thermoplastic that is often used as the build material or 'filament' in thermoplastic extrusion.

ADDITIVE MANUFACTURING

Additive manufacturing (AM) is the process of building up an object in a great many very thin layers. 3D printing is therefore an additive manufacturing process. Engineers often refer to 3D printing as additive manufacturing, although increasingly the two terms are used interchangeably.

ADDITIVE METAL MANUFACTURING

Additive metal manufacturing (AMM) refers to any 3D printing technology that builds up metal objects in layers. Most usually the label is used to collectively refer to powder-based technologies such as direct metal laser sintering (DMLS), laserCUSING, electron beam melting (EBM) and directed energy deposition. However, it may also include the fused deposition modelling of metals (FDMm) as achieved via wire and arc manufacturing (WAAM).

ALUMIDE

Alumide is a 3D printing material that is a two-part mix of plastic powder and aluminium. It is used in 3D printers based on selective laser sintering (SLS) to produce objects with a metal feel and sparkle at relatively low cost.

AM

See additive manufacturing.

AMM

See additive metal manufacturing.

AUTOCAD

AutoCAD is a leading computer aided design (CAD) program from Autodesk that is widely used to create digital 3D objects that may then be 3D printed.

BINDER JETTING

Binder jetting is a generic label for 3D printing technologies that spray a binder from an inkjet-style print head onto successive layers of powder. ZPrinters from 3D Systems achieve full-colour binder jetting by spraying coloured inks as well as a binder onto successive layers of a gypsum-based powder. Other companies produce binder jetting 3D printers that bond ceramic, plastic or metal powders.

BIO-INK

Bio-ink is a culture of living cells used as the build material in a bioprinter. The term was coined by bioprinting pioneer Organovo, who load their bioprinters with 'bio-ink spheroids' that each contain tens of thousands of cells.

BIO-PAPER

Bio-paper is the support material used by a bioprinter, and is usually a hydrogel, such as a water-collagen mix. The term was coined by bioprinting pioneer Organovo, whose bioprinters place 'bio-ink spheroids' into successive bio-paper layers to 3D print living tissue.

BIOPRINTER

A bioprinter is a 3D printer that outputs objects made of living cells, rather than plastics, metals or other inorganic materials.

BREAKAWAY SUPPORT TECHNOLOGY

Breakaway support technology (BST) is featured on 3D printers that add extra build material to an object during printout to hold in place upward sloping or potentially 'orphan' parts that would otherwise fall away. Breakaway supports are a feature of stereolithographic and single-material thermoplastic extrusion 3D printers, and have to be removed by hand after printout. Additional object clean-up (such as sanding) is sometimes required to remove evidence of where breakaway supports were attached.

BST

See breakaway support technology.

CNC

CNC stands for 'computer numerical control'. CNC machine tools that allow digital designs to be automatically crafted are now common in many factories and workshops.

CONCEPT MODEL

A concept model is a physical representation of a final product that approximates its form, but which lacks the final object's functionality and material characteristics. Concept models are created by designers to allow them to communicate their ideas to clients and to assess how a design is evolving. Increasingly, concept models are being produced using 3D printers.

CUBE
Cube is the name of a range of thermoplastic extrusion 3D printers produced by 3D Systems Corporation. The first Cube model was launched in January 2012 as the first truly consumer 3D printer. Further models were launched in 2013.

CUBIFY
Cubify is a website run by 3D Systems Corporation that sells and supports its Cube 3D printers. The site also provides an online 3D printing service, offers a range of 3D objects for sale, and facilitates a 3D printing community.

DDM
See direct digital manufacturing.

DIRECT DIGITAL MANUFACTURING
Direct digital manufacturing (DDM) refers to the production of final products, or parts thereof, using a 3D printer.

DIRECT METAL LASER SINTERING
Direct metal laser sintering (DMLS) is a powder fed fusion 3D printing technology that uses a laser to selectively heat and so fuse together successive layers of a metal powder. Common build materials used in DMLS include aluminium, steel, nickel alloys, cobalt chrome, iron and titanium.

DIRECTED ENERGY DEPOSITION
Directed energy deposition is the generic name for a 3D

printing technology that deposits metal powders from a print head and fuses them together using a laser or another controllable heat source. The technology has been pioneered by Optomec – who refer to it as 'laser engineered net shaping' (LENS) – and can be used to both fabricate and repair metal components.

DLP PROJECTION

DLP projection is a 3D printing technology based on photopolymerization. In a DLP projection 3D printer, a DLP or 'digital light processing' projector is focused on the surface of a tank of photocurable polymer. Light from the projector then solidifies a complete layer of an object. The object is then lowered slightly so that the projector can solidify another layer, and so on.

DMLS

See direct metal laser sintering.

DOD

See drop on demand.

DROP ON DEMAND

Drop on demand (DOD) is a material extrusion 3D printing process used to create dental wax-ups and other sacrificial molds or patterns out of a special casting material. It was created by a company called Solidscape that is now owned by Stratasys.

EBF3

See electron beam melting.

EBM

See electron beam melting

ELECTRON BEAM MELTING

Electron beam melting (EBM) is a powder bed fusion 3D printing technology that builds up metal objects in a vacuum by using an electron beam to selectively melt and so fuse together successive layers of a metal powder. Electron beam melting has been pioneered by a company called Arcam, and is restricted in its application to high value metals such as titanium and cobalt chrome. NASA has also experimented with EBM, with its engineers having termed the technology 'electron beam free form fabrication', or EBF3.

FAB@HOME

Fab@Home is an open source 3D printer that uses one or more syringe tools to build objects via material extrusion. Materials that can be printed with a Fab@Home printer include epoxy resin, silicone rubber, cake frosting, cheese, PlayDoh, ceramic clay and gypsum plaster. The project was started in 2006 by Hod Lipson and Evan Malone, and is run from the Computational Synthesis Laboratory at Cornell University.

FDC

See fused deposition of ceramics.

FDM

See fused deposition modelling.

FDMM

See fused deposition modelling of metals.

FFF

See fused filament fabrication.

FFM

See fused filament modelling.

FILAMENT

Filament is the material used to 3D print objects via material extrusion, also commonly referred to as 'fused deposition modelling' (FDM). Filament is typically a thermoplastic (such as ABS or PLA) that is fed to a print head as a solid, and then heated for extrusion from a small nozzle. Filament is typically 3 mm or 1.75 mm in diameter, and is purchased on spools.

FUNCTIONAL PROTOTYPE

A functional prototype is a representation of a final product created during the design process to test the form, fit and function of the intended object and its constituent parts. Functional prototypes need not necessarily be built from the same materials that will be used to make the final product. For example, engine parts may be 3D printed in plastic to test how they fit and move together before final parts are produced in metal.

FUSED DEPOSITION MODELLING

Fused deposition modelling (FDM) is a material extrusion 3D printing process that creates objects in layers by depositing a heated thermoplastic from a computer-controlled print head nozzle. FDM was invented by a company called Stratasys, which has trademarked the term. Other companies subsequently refer to this kind of technology as 'plastic jet printing' (PJP), 'fused filament modelling' (FFM), 'fused filament fabrication' (FFF), the 'fused deposition method', or simply 'thermoplastic extrusion'.

FUSED DEPOSITION MODELLING OF METALS

The fused deposition modelling of metals (FDMm) is a form of material extrusion or 'fused deposition modelling' (FDM) that deposits a molten metal to 3D print objects in successive layers. *See also* wire and arc additive manufacturing (WAAM).

FUSED DEPOSITION OF CERAMICS

The fused deposition of ceramics (FDC) refers to the 3D printing of ceramic objects using multiphase jet solidification (MJS).

FUSED FILAMENT FABRICATION

Fused filament fabrication (FFF) is another term for thermoplastic extrusion, which is also commonly referred to as fused deposition modelling (FDM).

FUSED FILAMENT MODELLING

Fused filament modelling (FFM) is another term for thermoplastic extrusion, which is also commonly referred to as fused deposition modelling (FDM).

GRANULAR MATERIALS BINDING

Granular materials binding is a generic term for all forms of 3D printing that create objects by laying down successive layers of power and selectively sticking their granules together. Granular materials binding therefore encompasses a wide range of technologies, including binder jetting, 3D sand casting, selective laser sintering (SLS), selective laser melting (SLM), direct metal laser sintering (DMLS), selective heat sintering (SHS), laserCUSING and electron beam melting (EBM).

I.MATERIALISE

i.materialise is an online service that allows anybody to upload, 3D print and sell their designs in a wide range of materials. i.materialise is part of a wider 3D printing company called Materialise and is based in Leuven in Belgium.

LAMINATED OBJECT MANUFACTURE

Laminated object manufacture (LOM) is a 3D printing technology that builds up objects by adhering together successive sheets of laser cut paper, plastic or metal foil. The technology is also sometimes termed 'sheet lamination'.

LASER ENGINEERED NET SHAPING

Laser engineered net shaping (LENS) is a directed energy deposition 3D printing technology pioneered and trademarked by a company called Optomec.

LASER POWDER FORMING

Laser powder forming is another term for the directed energy deposition process that builds objects by supplying a metal powder to a print head and melting it with a laser.

LASERCUSING

LaserCUSING is a 3D printing technology that uses high power lasers positioned close to a powder bed to selectively fuse together the granules of a metal build material. The technology is optimized to produce final parts with a homogenous material structure.

LAYWOO-3D

LAYWOO-3D is a composite of wood fibres and a polymer binder that can be used as the build material (filament) in a material extrusion 3D printer to build wooden objects.

LDM

See low-temperature deposition modelling.

LENS

See laser engineered net shaping *and* directed energy deposition.

LOM
See laminated object manufacture.

LOW-TEMPERATURE DEPOSITION MODELLING
Low-temperature deposition modelling (LDM) is a form of material extrusion or 'fused deposition modelling' (FDM) that works at low temperatures, and which has particular potential application in tissue engineering.

MATERIAL EXTRUSION
Material extrusion is the generic term for any 3D printing technology that builds objects in layers by extruding a material – such as a molten thermoplastic – from a computer-controlled print head nozzle. Many people refer to material extrusion as fused deposition modelling (FDM), although this label has been trademarked by a 3D printer manufacturer called Stratasys. Other terms used to refer to material extrusion include thermoplastic extrusion, fused filament modelling (FFM), fused filament fabrication (FFF) and plastic jet printing (PJP).

MATERIAL JETTING
Material jetting is the generic name for any 3D printing technology that emits a liquid photopolymer from a print head. After each layer of material has been printed, it is rapidly set solid with UV light before the next layer is printed on top of it. Such photopolymer material jetting is known within the 3D printing industry via a variety of other names, including 'polyjet' (short for 'photopolymer jet'), 'PolyJet Matrix' (a term trademarked by Stratasys), 'multi jet modelling' (MJM), or 'inkjet photopolymer printing'.

MJS
See multiphase jet solidification.

MULTIPHASE JET SOLIDIFICATION

Multiphase jet solidification (MJS) is a 3D printing process where a ceramic or metal powder is mixed with a binder so that it can be heated and extruded into object layers via a method similar to material extrusion. Once an object has been created, the binder needs to be removed thermally (ie by heating it so that it drains away) or chemically (by immersing the object in an appropriate solvent). Final objects then need to be 'densified' by intense heating in a kiln.

OBJET

Objet was a pioneering Israeli 3D printing company that invented and successfully commercialized a material jetting technology that it called PolyJet Matrix. This mixes different photopolymers together as each object layer is built, so allowing 14 different materials to be printed at the same time. The company merged with Stratasys in December 2012, and ceased to trade under the name Objet in early 2013.

ORGANOVO

Organovo is a 3D printing pioneer that is working to create human tissue and transplantable organs using bioprinters.

PATTERN

A pattern is a master version of an object created for the purposes of taking a mold. Traditionally patterns have been time consuming and costly to produce. However, they can now be created using a variety of 3D printing techniques.

PHOTOPOLYMER

Photopolymers are plastic resins that change their properties when exposed to light. Liquid photopolymers that rapidly solidify when exposed to ultraviolet (UV) light are used as the build material in stereolithographic, material jetting,

DLP projection and two-photon polymerization 3D printers.

PHOTOPOLYMERIZATION
Photopolymerization is the generic name for all 3D printing technologies that use a laser or other light source to selectively solidify a liquid photopolymer build material. Such technologies include stereolithography, DLP projection, two-photon polymerization (2PP) and material jetting.

PJP
See plastic jet printing.

PLA
See polylactic acid.

PLASTIC JET PRINTING
Plastic jet printing (PJP) is a 3D printing technology that builds objects in layers by extruding a molten thermoplastic from a print head nozzle. The term is used by 3D Systems Corporation, and is another term for thermoplastic extrusion or fused deposition modelling (FDM).

POLYJET
Polyjet is a common term for 'material jetting', and refers to a photopolymerization 3D printing technology where objects are built by spraying a liquid photopolymer from a print head, with each layer then solidified with UV light before the next is printed.

POLYLACTIC ACID
Polylactic acid (PLA) is a bioplastic that can be used as the build material or 'filament' in thermoplastic extrusion.

POWDER BED FUSION

Powder bed fusion is a generic term for any 3D printing technology that builds objects in layers by using a heat source to selectively stick together successive layers of powder. Power bed fusion therefore encompasses overlapping technologies including selective laser sintering (SLS), selective laser melting (SLM), selective heat sintering (SHS), direct metal laser sintering (DMLS), electron beam melting (EBM) and laserCUSING.

RAPID PROTOTYPING

Rapid prototyping (RP) refers to any technology used to create a prototype object from digital data using computer-controlled hardware. For many years 3D printers were referred to as rapid prototypers, as this was almost entirely what they were used for. However, 3D printers are now used for far more than rapid prototyping. Other non-3D-printing hardware – such as computer numerically controlled (CNC) machine tools – may also be used to create rapid prototypes. Rapid prototyping and 3D printing are hence not entirely interchangeable terms and ought not to be confused.

REPRAP

RepRaps – or 'replicating rapid prototypers' – are open source, thermoplastic extrusion 3D printers capable of printing out many of their own parts. A range of different RepRap designs and build instructions can be freely downloaded from RepRap.org, where the printers are described as 'humanity's first general-purpose self-replicating manufacturing machines'.

RP

See rapid prototyping.

SACRIFICIAL MOLD

A sacrificial mold is a single-use item that is destroyed during the production process that utilizes it. For example, sacrificial molds made from sand are used in industrial 'sand casting'. Here a molten metal is poured into a 'sand cast' comprised of sand and a special resin. Once the metal has cooled solid, the sand cast is then 'sacrificed' as it is broken away.

SELECTIVE HEAT SINTERING

Selective heat sintering (SHS) is a powder bed fusion 3D printing technology created by a company called BluePrinter. The process is similar to selective laser sintering (SLS), but uses a thermal print head rather than a laser to selectively fuse together successive layers of a plastic powder.

SELECTIVE LASER MELTING

Selective laser melting (SLM) is a powder bed fusion 3D printing technology that is similar to selective laser sintering (SLS), but which uses a higher power laser to entirely melt the powder granules that are selectively fused together to create metal objects.

SELECTIVE LASER SINTERING

Selective laser sintering (SLS) is a powder bed fusion 3D printing technology that uses a laser to selectively fuse or 'sinter' together the granules of successive layers of powder.

SHAPEWAYS

Shapeways is a 3D printing marketplace, community and online 3D printing service that allows designers to share their designs and anybody to get things printed out.

SHEET LAMINATION

Sheet lamination is a 3D printing technology that builds up

objects by adhering together successive sheets of laser cut paper, plastic or metal foil. The technology is more commonly known as laminated object manufacture (LOM).

SHS
See selective heat sintering

SINTERING
Sintering is a process that heats the outsides of particles of powder in order to fuse them together.

SKETCHUP
SketchUp is a computer aided design (CAD) program that can be used to create digital models for 3D printing. The software comes in two versions – a personal edition which is free to download, and a paid professional edition. SketchUp was for a while a Google product, though was sold to Trimble Navigation in April 2012.

SL
See stereolithography.

SLA
See stereolithography.

SLM
See selective laser melting.

SLS
See selective laser sintering.

SOLIDWORKS
SolidWorks is a leading 3D computer aided design (CAD) program from Dassault Systèmes.

SOLUBLE SUPPORT TECHNOLOGY

Soluble support technology (SST) is featured on 3D printers that output a dissolvable material during printout to hold in place the upward sloping or potentially 'orphan' parts of an object that would otherwise fall away. As the name suggests, soluble supports are removed after printout using a liquid solvent (such as a water-based detergent) that is either jetted onto an object, or agitated around it in a special tank.

SST

See soluble support technology.

STEREOLITHOGRAPHY

Stereolithography (SL) is a 3D printing technology that builds up objects in layers using a so-termed StereoLithographic Apparatus (SLA). Stereolithography is based on photopolymerization, with a laser beam used to trace out and solidify each successive layer of an object on the surface of a vat of liquid photopolymer.

STL

STL is a computer file format widely used in 3D printing. The format was created in 1987 as a means of translating computer aided design (CAD) files for printout using the first commercial stereolithographic 3D printers created by 3D Systems. Today, most 3D printers create objects from STL files, regardless of the technology they are based on. Exactly what STL is an acronym for is debated, though most commonly it is taken to be short for 'standard tessellation language'.

STRATASYS

Stratasys is a leading 3D printer manufacturer and service provider focused on high-end industrial and commercial clients and applications.

SUPPORT STRUCTURE

Support structures are additional parts that are added to objects during 3D printing to prevent overhanging or orphan (disconnected) parts falling away. *See also* breakaway support technology (BST) *and* soluble support technology (SST).

THERMOPLASTIC

A thermoplastic is a plastic whose shape can be changed by heating it into a molten form and then allowing it to cool back into a solid. Thermoplastics are widely used as the build material (filament) in thermoplastic extrusion 3D printing, otherwise known as fused deposition modelling (FDM).

THERMOPLASTIC EXTRUSION

Thermoplastic extrusion is a 3D printing process that creates objects in layers by extruding a heated thermoplastic from a computer-controlled print head nozzle. The technology is also widely known by other terms, including 'fused deposition modelling' (FDM), 'plastic jet printing' (PJP), 'fused filament modelling' (FFM), 'fused filament fabrication' (FFF), and the 'fused deposition method'.

THINGIVERSE

Thingiverse is a website that allows people to upload and share digital designs that can be downloaded for 3D printing.

TISSUE ENGINEERING

Tissue engineering refers to the creation or alteration of living matter, as may be achieved using a bioprinter.

TWO-PHOTON POLYMERIZATION

Two-photon polymerization (2PP) is an experimental 3D printing technology similar to stereolithography. The technology uses a femtosecond pulsed laser to selectively solidify successive layers of a specially developed liquid photopolymer that includes 'initiator' molecules that trigger monomer solidification when stuck by two photons. Two-photon polymerization is potentially revolutionary because it can achieve a layer thickness and an X-Y axes accuracy down to 100 nanometres (0.0001 mm), making it several hundred times more accurate that other 3D printing methods.

VAT PHOTOPOLYMERIZATION
Vat photopolymerization is a generic term for any form of 3D printing in which a vat or tank of liquid photopolymer is selectively solidified using a laser beam or other light source. Vat photopolymerization technologies currently include stereolithography, DLP projection and two-photon polymerization (2PP).

WAAM
See wire and arc additive manufacturing.

WIRE AND ARC ADDITIVE MANUFACTURING
Wire and arc additive manufacturing (WAAM) is an experimental form of 3D printing based on the fused deposition modelling of metals (FDMm). The technology uses an adapted arc fusion welding robot, and feeds a thin titanium wire to the tip of a robotic arm where it is melted for deposition into object layers.

3D PRINTING DIRECTORY

3D printing is now evolving extremely quickly. This directory includes those 3D printer manufacturers, software vendors, bureau services, and online information sources, that I could readily identify at the time of publication. A constantly updated version of this directory can be accessed from http://explainingthefuture.com/3dprinting.

3D PRINTER MANUFACTURERS – INDUSTRIAL

The following all manufacture 3D printers for commercial applications that range from rapid prototyping to direct digital manufacturing (DDM):

3D SYSTEMS – http://www.3dsystems.com

3D Systems Corporation is the largest 3D printer manufacturer, and makes hardware for both high-end industrial clients and end consumers. The company's 3D printer models are based on a wide range of technologies, including stereolithography, binder jetting, material jetting, laser sintering and thermoplastic extrusion. 3D Systems has grown rapidly by acquiring other 3D printer manufacturers, including Z Corporation and Bits From Bytes.

ARCAM – http://arcam.com

Arcam produces 3D printers based on its electron beam melting (EBM) technology. This allows fully-dense metal parts to be produced for medical implant, aerospace and defence applications.

ASIGA – https://www.asiga.com

Asiga produces high-resolution, sub-$7,000 desktop stereo-lithographic 3D printers. Their hardware has a 'pico' build volume intended to accommodate the production of dental pieces, jewelry and similar small items.

BLUEPRINTER – http://www.blueprinter.dk

Blueprinter produces a desktop 3D printer that uses its own selective heat sintering (SHS) technology to build objects out of a thermoplastic powder.

CONCEPT LASER – http://www.concept-laser.de

Concept Laser produce 3D printers based on their unique laserCUSING technology. This very accurately produces object layers from metal powders for aerospace, automotive, medical, dental and other industrial applications.

ENVISIONTEC – http://www.envisiontec.de

EnvisionTEC produce a range of photopolymerization 3D printers that are used for a wide variety of dental, medical, mold making, prototyping and other applications. The company also sells its 3D-Bioplotter for tissue engineering (bioprinting).

EOS – http://www.eos.info

EOS manufactures a range of industrial selective laser sinter-ing (SLS) 3D printers, with different models available that are dedicated to making things in metals, plastics or sand (for 3D sand casting).

EXONE – http://www.exone.com

ExOne sells industrial 3D printers that use binder jetting to build objects in sand (to enable 3D sand casting), as well as stainless steel, bronze and glass.

MCOR TECHNOLOGIES – http://mcortechnologies.com

Mcor Technologies makes 3D printers that use laminated object manufacture (LOM) and inkjet technology to produce full-colour 3D objects using standard copier paper.

NANOSCRIBE – http://www.nanoscribe.de/en

Nanoscribe produce a nanolithograhic 3D printer that uses two-photon polymerization (2PP) to create 3D objects on a nanoscale.

OPTOMEC – http://www.optomec.com

Optomec produces 3D printers based on its 'laser engineered net shaping' (LENS) technology that deposits a metal powder that is melted with a laser to produce fully-dense, end-use metal parts. The company also sells 'Aerosol Jet' hardware that can print working electronics onto 3D surfaces.

ORGANOVO – http://www.organovo.com

Organovo are a bioprinting pioneer who produce a 3D bio-printer called the Novogen MMX.

SLM SOLUTIONS – http://www.slm-solutions.com

SLM Solutions produce a range of 3D printers that build objects from powders using selective laser melting (SLM).

SOLIDO3D – http://www.solido3d.com

Solido3D makes 3D printers that use laminated object manufacture (LOM) to produce 3D objects from sheets of plastic.

STRATASYS – http://www.stratasys.com

Stratasys is the second-largest 3D printer manufacturer, and makes 3D printers that use fused deposition modelling (FDM) or PolyJet Matrix (material jetting) technologies. The company's PolyJet Matrix 'Connex' range can print in 14 materials at the same time, and entered the Stratasys fold after the company's merger with the Israeli 3D printer manufacturer Objet in January 2013. In addition to hardware sold under its own name, Stratasys also markets Mojo, Dimension, Fortus and uPrint 3D printers.

VOXELJET – http://www.voxeljet.de/en
Voxeljet produces a range of 3D printers that use binder jetting to produce either plastic objects or 3D sand castings from powders. The company's largest model – the VX4000 – has an incredible build volume of 4 x 2 x 1 m (about 13.1 x 6.5 x 3.3 feet).

3D PRINTER MANUFACTURERS – PERSONAL
The following are just some of the companies that sell 3D printers (and 3D printer kits) with a smaller price tag, and which are intended for personal/desktop use. Some of these models do, nevertheless, have the potential for small-scale commercial application:

CB-PRINTER – http://cb-printer.com
CB-printer is the first domestic 3D printer to be produced in Poland. Its '3D Printer CB-printer' is available either fully assembled or as a kit.

CUBIFY – http://cubify.com
Cubify is part of 3D Systems Corporation, and sells several thermoplastic extrusion, consumer-grade 3D printers. These range from a single-material 'Cube', to the larger, multi-material 'Cube X Duo' and 'Cube X Trio'.

DELTA MICRO FACTORY CORP – http://pp3dp.com

The Delta Micro Factory Corporation is a Chinese 3D printer manufacturer. Under their PP3DP brand, the company sells the UP! range of low-cost, desktop 3D printers which use thermoplastic extrusion to build plastic objects. The same printers are also imported into the United States and resold by a company called Afinia (http://www.afinia.com).

FORMLABS – http://formlabs.com

Formlabs produces a low-cost desktop stereolithographic printer called the Form 1.

MAKEGEAR – http://www.makergear.com

MakerGear develops products and services for the maker community, and sells its own M2 thermoplastic extrusion 3D printers in both kit and fully-assembled formats. Maker-Gear also sell some RepRap open source 3D printer models.

MAKERBOT INDUSTRIES – http://www.makerbot.com

MakerBot produces a range of low-cost, desktop 3D printers that use thermoplastic extrusion to create plastic objects. The company claims around a 20 per cent share of all 3D printers sold.

PORTABEE – http://portabee3dprinter.com

The Portabee is a small, low-cost and foldable thermoplastic extrusion 3D printer available either fully assembled or as a kit.

PRINTRBOT – http://www.printrbot.com

Printerbot produces very low cost 3D printers in both kit-form and fully assembled. The company's printers are based on thermoplastic extrusion, and have iconic laser-cut-plywood body panels.

REPRAPPRO – http://www.reprappro.com
RepRapPro sell a wide range of kits for building open source RepRap 3D printers based on thermoplastic extrusion.

REPRAPUNIVERSE.COM – http://reprapuniverse.com
ReprapUniverse.com sells kits for MendleMax and Prussa open source RepRap 3D printers.

SOLIDOODLE – http://www.solidoodle.com
Solidoodle is a fully-assembled, low-cost thermoplastic extrusion 3D printer available in 'base', 'pro' and 'expert' versions.

ULTIMAKER – http://www.ultimaker.com
The Ultimaker 3D printer is a lightweight, robust and very-well-respected piece of thermoplastic extrusion hardware. In comparative tests, the Ultimaker frequently beats all rivals on the basis of its speed and quality of output.

3D PRINTING DESIGN SOFTWARE
The following can all be used to produce digital objects for 3D printout:

AUTOCAD – http://usa.autodesk.com/autocad-products
AutoCAD is a high-end, industry leading CAD package from Autodesk in which many 3D printed objects are digitally created.

AUTODESK 123D – http://www.123dapp.com
Autodesk 123D is a range of free 3D printing design applications.

CUBIFY INVENT – http://cubify.com/products/cubify_invent
Cubify Invent is an entry-level modelling package from 3D

Systems that is written from the ground up for those wishing to create objects for 3D printout.

SKETCHUP – http://www.sketchup.com

SketchUp (formerly Google SketchUp) is a popular 3D modelling application from Trimble Navigation. The software comes in two versions – a personal edition which is free to download, and a paid professional edition.

SOLIDWORKS – http://www.solidworks.com

SolidWorks is a highly popular, professional CAD package from Dassault Systèmes that is frequently used to produce models for 3D printout.

TURBOCAD – http://www.turbocad.com

TurboCAD is a popular and relatively-low-cost design package that can be used to create objects for 3D printout.

3D PRINTING BUREAU

The following are just some of the companies that offer 3D printing and related services:

3D CREATION LAB – http://www.3dcreationlab.co.uk

Based in Staffordshire in the UK, 3D Creation Lab offers a range of material jetting, thermoplastic extrusion and colour binder jetting 3D printing services.

3D PRINT UK – http://www.3dprint-uk.co.uk

3D Print UK is a London-based company that offers a range of design, CAD and 3D printing services.

3DPROPARTS – http://www.3dproparts.com

3Dproparts offers an overnight service for the production of prototypes, production parts and production tooling in a wide range of materials. The company is part of the US 3D printing giant 3D Systems Corporation.

3T RPD LTD – http://www.3trpd.co.uk

3T RPD Ltd uses laser sintering to manufacture plastic or metal parts, and is one of the largest providers of such a service in the United Kingdom.

DRAFT PRINT 3D – http://www.draftprint3d.com

Draft Print is a UK provider of 3D design and scanning services, as well as thermoplastic extrusion 3D printing.

FIGULO – http://figulo.com/figulo

Based in Boston, MA, Figulo provides an online service that allows uploaded objects to be 3D printed in ceramics.

FIT PRODUCTION – http://www.fit-production.de

FIT Production is a German provider of 3D printing services for a wide range of industrial applications.

GROWIT – http://www.growit3d.com

GROWit is a CAD engineering, 3D scanning and 3D printing service based in Lake Forest, CA. The company utilizes material jetting, thermoplastic extrusion, binder jetting and laser sintering technologies to create both proto-types and final product parts.

I.MATERIALISE – http://i.materialise.com

i.materialise is part of the wider Materialise group based in Leuven in Belgium. It offers a worldwide online 3D printing service, allowing customers to upload models for printout in a wide 'Periodic Table of Materials'. Designers can also use i.materialise to sell their creations online via print-on-demand.

INITION – http://inition.co.uk

Inition offers a 3D scanning and 3D printing bureau service, as well as working in 3D media production.

LPE – http://www.laserproto.com

LPE (Laser Prototypes Europe Limited) was the first rapid prototyping service bureau in the UK and Ireland, and can 3D print objects using stereolithography or selective laser sintering.

PONOKO – https://www.ponoko.com

With offices in Germany, Italy, New Zealand, the UK and the US, Ponoko offers a 'personal factory service' that includes online 3D printing, laser cutting and CNC routing.

PRINT TO 3D – http://www.printo3d.com

Print To 3D is based in Tunkhannock, PA, and can 3D print objects using thermoplastic extrusion.

PROTO3000 – http://proto3000.com

Proto3000 is based in Montreal, and can produce prototypes, tooling and other objects using all major 3D printing technologies. The company also offers 3D scanning, design and product development services.

RAPIDO3D – http://rapido3d.co.uk

Rapido3D offers a range of 3D printing, 3D scanning and related services.

SCULPTEO – http://www.sculpteo.com

Sculpteo describes itself as the '3D Printing Cloud Engine', and provides an online 3D printing service that allows anybody to upload 3D models and get them printed out in a wide variety of materials. Designers can also open up a store to sell their creations via print-on-demand. Sculpteo is head-quartered in France, but has a US office in San Francisco.

SHAPEWAYS – http://www.shapeways.com
Shapeways is a leading global online 3D printing bureau that allows anybody to upload objects for 3D printout using all available technologies. Designers can also open up a 'Shape-ways shop' that allows them to sell their designs via print-on-demand. Sometimes termed the 'Amazon of 3D printing', Shapeways was founded in the Netherlands but is now head-quartered in New York.

3D PRINTING NEWS & INFORMATION
The following are my top recommendations for the latest online information on 3D printing:

3D PRINTING INDUSTRY – http://3dprintingindustry.com

3D PRINTING IS THE FUTURE – http://3dfuture.com.au

3D PRINTING NEWS – http://www.3dprintingnews.co.uk

3DERS.ORG – http://www.3ders.org

3DPRINTING.COM – http://3dprinting.com

3DPRINTER.NET – http://www.3dprinter.net

REPLICATOR WORLD – http://www.replicatorworld.com

THE FUTURE IS 3D – http://thefutureis3d.com

FURTHER READING

CHAPTER 1: THE NEXT REVOLUTION

Liat Clark 'Airbus Designer Reveals Plans for 3D Printed Planes by 2050', *Wired* (12 July 2012). Available from: http://www.wired.co.uk/news/archive/2012-07/12/3d-printed-plane-by-2050

Gerald Ferreira 'In Transit to 3D Printing Boom: Ford a Major Player in Digital Revolution', 3DCarShows.com (no date). Available from: http://3d-car-shows.com/2012/in-transit-to-3d-printing-boom-ford-a-major-player-in-digital-revolution/

Martin Hearn 'Voxeljet 3D Printer Used to Produce Skyfall's Aston Martin Stunt Double', *Engadget* (12 November 2012). Available from: http://www.engadget.com/2012/11/12/voxeljet-3d-printer-skyfalls-aston-martin-stunt-double/

Tony Smith 'Japan Firm Offers Mums-to-be 3D Printed Unborn Infants', *The Register* (28 November 2012). Available from: http://www.theregister.co.uk/2012/11/28/japanese_firm_fasotec_offers_3d_printed_embryos/

Joel Willans 'Everything You Need to Know About the Lumia 820 and 3D Printing', (Nokia, 18 January 2013). Available from: http://conversations.nokia.com/2013/01/18/everything-you-need-to-know-about-the-lumia-820-and-3d-printing/

CHAPTER 2: 3D PRINTING TECHNOLOGIES

3D Printer Hub 'Resin and Mirrors: Breakthrough Research Speeds 3D Printing by Orders of Magnitude' (18 March 2012). Available from:

http://3dprinterhub.com/3d-printer-news/resin-and-mirrors-break-through-research-speeds-3d-printing-by-orders-of-magnitude/146

3Ders.org 'LAYWOO-D3: New FDM Filament Can Print Wood with Tree Rings' (20 September 2012). Available from: http://www.3ders.org/articles/20120920-laywoo-d3-new-fdm-filament-can-print-wood-with-tree-rings.html

3Ders.org 'Microscale Printing of a Spaceship on World's Fastest 3D Printer' (9 February 2013). Available from: http://www.3ders.org/articles/20130209-microscale-printing-of-a-spaceship-on-worlds-fastest-3d-printer.html

Tim Adams 'The "Chemputer" That Could Print Any Drug', *The Guardian* (21 July 2012). Available from: http://www.guardian.co.uk/science/2012/jul/21/chemputer-that-prints-out-drugs

Anna Bellini, Lauren Shor, Selcuk I. Guceri, 'New Developments in Fused Deposition Modeling of Ceramics', *Rapid Prototyping Journal* (2005, Volume 11 Issue 4).

Tom Cheshire 'BurritoB0t: The 3D Printer that Creates Mexican Snacks in Five Minutes', *Wired* (16 August 2012). Available from: http://www.wired.co.uk/magazine/archive/2012/09/play/press-print-to-pig-out

Daniel Cooper 'What's Past is Prologue: a Look Inside the Future of Lockheed Martin', *Engadget* (29 November 2012). Available from: http://www.engadget.com/2012/11/29/lockheed-martin

Thomas Frey 'Printable Houses and the Future Opportunity Therein', *The Futurist* – Thomas Frey's Blog (10 April 2012). Available from: http://www.wfs.org/content/printable-houses-and-future-opportunity-therein

Joe Hiemenz '3D Printing with FDM', (Stratasys, no date). Available from: http://www.stratasys.com/~/Media/Main/Files/White%20Papers/SSYS-WP-3DP-HowItWorks-09-11.aspx

John Newman 'Standardizing Additive Manufacturing Process Terminology', *Rapid Ready Technology* (13 June 2012). Available from: http://www.rapidreadytech.com/2012/06/the-art-of-simplicity-standardized-process-terminology

CHAPTER 3: THE 3D PRINTING INDUSTRY

Mark Fleming 'Investing in 3D printing Stocks in 2013', *3DPrinter.net* (21 January 2013). Available from: http://www.3dprinter.net/investing-in-3d-printing-stocks-in-2013

Markets and Markets *Additive Manufacturing Market (2012 - 2017), By Application (Medical Devices, Automotives, & Aerospace) and Technology (3D Printing, Laser Sintering, Stereolithography, Fused Deposition Modeling, Electron Beam Melting, & Tissue Engineering)* (October 2012). Available via: http://www.marketsandmarkets.com/Market-Reports/additive-manufacturing-medical-devices-market-843.html

Terry Wohlers *Wohlers Report 2012*, (Wohlers Associates, 2012). Available via: http://wohlersassociates.com/press56.htm

CHAPTER 4: DIGITAL MANUFACTURING PIONEERS

Doug Bartholomew 'Additive Manufacturing Goes Mainstream', *Industry Week* (March 10 2012). Available from: http://www.industryweek.com/articles/additive_manufacturing_goes_mainstream_26805.aspx?page=2

Avi Cohen 'Digital Dentistry Makes an Impression', *Today's Medical Developments* (April 2012). Available from: http://www.onlinetmd.com/tmd0412-dentistry-3d-printing-technology.aspx

Clay Dillow 'UK Engineers Print and Fly the World's First Working 3-D Printed Aircraft', *Popsci* (28 July 2011). Available from: http://www.popsci.com/technology/article/2011-07/uk-engineers-print-and-fly-worlds-first-working-3-d-printed-aircraft?cmp=tw

Joris Peels 'Shapeways Interviews Janne Kyttanen of FOC', *Shapeways Blog* (26 March 2010). Available from: http://www.shapeways.com/blog/archives/407-shapeways-interviews-janne-kyttanen-of-foc.html

Dina Spector 'Mining Company Will Use 3D Printer To Turn Raw Asteroids Into Valuable Metal Parts', *Business Insider* (22 January 2013). Available from: http://www.businessinsider.com/deep-space-industries-asteroid-mining-plans-2013-1

Eddie Wrenn 'From Dot Matrix to the Starting Grid: Racing Car Created by 3D Printer', *The Daily Mail* (28 August 2012). Available from:

http://www.dailymail.co.uk/sciencetech/article-2194626/From-dot-matrix-starting-grid-Racing-car-designed-purely-3D-printing-0-60mph-just-seconds.html

CHAPTER 5: PERSONAL FABRICATION

Sarah Boisvert 'The coming Industrial Revolution is a Lot Bigger Than Just 3D Printing' (interview with Neil Gershenfeld) *3DPrinter.net* (23 January 2013). Available from: http://www.3dprinter.net/coming-industrial-revolution-bigger-than-3d-printing

Lemon Curry *Open Source UV Photopolymer DLP 3D Printer wiki.* (4 March 2013). Available from: https://code.google.com/p/lemoncurry/wiki/main

Andy Greenberg 'Inside Thingiverse, The Radically Open Website Powering The 3D Printing Movement', *Forbes* (10 December 2012). Also available via http://www.forbes.com

Andy Ide 'Interview with Dr Adrian Bowyer', *3D Printing is the Future* (no date). Available from: http://www.3dfuture.com.au/interview-with-dr-adrian-bowyer-the-creator-of-the-reprap-3d-printer/

Make Magazine *Make Ultimate Guide to 3D Printing* (O'Reilly, Winter 2013).

Technopedia *Maker Movement* (no date). Available from: http://www.techopedia.com/definition/28408/maker-movement

Audrey Watters 'Top Ed-Tech Trends of 2012: The Maker Movement', *Hack Education* (21 November 2012). Available from: http://hackeducation.com/2012/11/21/top-ed-tech-trends-of-2012-maker-movement/

CHAPTER 6: 3D PRINTING & SUSTAINABILITY

Christopher Barnatt *25 Things You Need to Know About the Future* (London: Constable, 2012).

Christopher Barnatt *Seven Ways to Fix the World* (ExplainingTheFuture.com, 2012).

BioInfoBank Library *Development of Aero Engine Component Manufacture using Laser Additive Manufacturing (MERLIN)* (21 September

2011). Available from: http://lib.bioinfo.pl/projects/view/22292

Census of Marine Life, The (4 October 2010). Available from: http://www.coml.org

Mark Fleming 'Dirk Vander Kooij's Incredible 3D Printed Furniture from Recycled e-Waste', *3DPrinter.net* (10 April 2013). Available from: http://www.3dprinter.net/dirk-vander-kooijs-3d-printed-furniture-from-e-waste

Jay Leno 'Jay Leno's 3D Printer Replaces Rusty Old Parts', *Popular Mechanics* (8 June 2009). Available from: http://www.popularmechanics.com/cars/jay-leno/technology/4320759

Hod Lipson & Melba Kurman *Fabricated: The New World of 3D Printing* (Indianapolis, IN: John Wiley & Sons, 2013).

Cameron Naramore '6 Ways 3D Printing Will Make the Future Sustainable', *3DPrinter.net* (11 November 2012). Available from: http://www.3dprinter.net/6-ways-3d-printing-will-make-the-future-sustainable

Stuart Nathan 'Printing Parts', *MIT Technology Review* (23 August 2011). Available from: http://www.technologyreview.com/demo/425133/printing-parts

SAVING Project, The: http://www.manufacturingthefuture.co.uk

Steve Sorrell, Jamie Speirs, Roger Bentley, Adam Brandt & Richard Miller *Global Oil Depletion: An Assessment of the Evidence for a Near-term Peak in Global Oil Production* (London: UK Energy Research Centre, 2009).

United Nations *Water Scarcity* (no date). Available from: http://www.un.org/waterforlifedecade/scarcity.shtml

United Nations Environment Programme *Uncoupling Natural Resource Use and Environmental Impacts from Economic Growth* (Washington, DC: United Nations, May 2011).

United Nations High Level Panel on Global Sustainability *Resilient People Resilient Planet: A Future Worth Choosing* (January 2012). Available from: http://www.un.org/gsp/sites/default/files/attachments/GSP_Report_web_final.pdf

CHAPTER 7: BIOPRINTING

Anthony Atala *Printing a Human Kidney*, 3 March 2011. Video available from: http://www.ted.com/talks/anthony_atala_printing_a_human_kidney.html

Christopher Barnatt *25 Things You Need to Know About the Future* (London: Constable, 2012).

Fabian Guillemot, Vladimir Mironov & Makoto Nakamura 'Editorial: Bioprinting is Coming of Age', *Biofabrication* (2010, Issue 2).

Richard Gray 'how a 3D Printer Gave Me Back My Face, and My Life', *The Sunday Telegraph* (31 March 2013).

Yuan Yuan Liu, Shu Hui Fang, Zhen Zhong Han, Ying Liu, Da Li Liu & Qing Xi Hu 'Study on Low-Temperature Deposition Manufacturing Process Parameters of Three-Dimensional Chitosan Scaffold', *Key Engineering Materials* (August 2012, Volume 522).

Vladimir Mironov 'The Future of Medicine: Are Custom-Printed Organs on the Horizon?' *The Futurist* (January–February 2011).

NHS Choices 'Woman Gets Artificial Jawbone Transplant' (7 February 2012). Available from: http://www.nhs.uk/news/2012/02February/Pages/3d-printing-jawbone-implant-created.aspx

Organovo *Organovo and OHSU Knight Cancer Institute Announce Collaboration in Cancer Research* (Press Release, 30 January 2013). Available from: http://investors.organovo.com/Newsroom/Press-Releases/Press-Releases-Details/2013/Organovo-and-OHSU-Knight-Cancer-Institute-Announce-Collaboration-in-Cancer-Research1133304/default.aspx

Organovo *Organovo Partners With Autodesk Research to Develop 3D Bioprinting Software* (Press Release, 18 December 2012). Available from: http://investors.organovo.com/Newsroom/Press-Releases/Press-Releases-Details/2012/Organovo-Partners-With-Autodesk-Research-to-Develop-3D-Bioprinting-Software1132373/default.aspx

Ibrahim Tarik Ozbolat & Howard Chen 'Manufacturing Living things', *Industrial Engineer* (January 2013).

CHAPTER 8: BRAVE NEW WORLD?

Engimaz '3D Printer DRM Patent To Stop People Downloading a Car', *Torrent Freak* (12 October 2012). Available from: http://torrentfreak. com/3d-printer-drm-patent-to-stop-people-downloading-a-car-121012/

Mark Fleming 'Stratasys Seizes 3D Printer From Printable Gun Project', *3Dprinter.net* (2 October 2012). Available from: http://www.3dprinter. net/defense-distributed-3d-printer-seized-by-stratasys

Thomas Frey 'Printable Houses and the Future Opportunity Therein', *The Futurist* – Thomas Frey's Blog (10 April 2012). Available from: http:// www.wfs.org/content/printable-houses-and-future-opportunity-therein

Andy Greenberg 'Inside Thingiverse, The Radically Open Website Powering The 3D Printing Movement', *Forbes* (21 November 2012). Available from: http://www.forbes.com/sites/andygreenberg/2012/11/21/inside-thingiverse-the-radically-open-website-powering-the-3d-printing-movement/

Ari Honka '3D Printed House – A Reality in Amsterdam?', *3Dprintingindustry.com* (14 March 2013). Available from http://3dprintingindustry.com/2013/03/14/3d-printed-house-a-reality-in-amsterdam

Richard Lai 'EADS's Airbike is a 3D-Printed Nylon Bicycle', *Engadget* (9 March 2011). Available from: http://www.engadget.com/2011/03/09/eadss-airbike-is-a-3d-printed-nylon-bicycle-actually-looks-rat/

Hod Lipson & Melba Kurman *Fabricated: The New World of 3D Printing* (Indianapolis, IN: John Wiley & Sons, 2013).

Joris Peels 'Shapeways Interviews Janne Kyttanen of FOC', *Shapeways Blog* (26 March 2010). Available from: http://www.shapeways.com/blog/archives/407-shapeways-interviews-janne-kyttanen-of-foc.html

Sustainable Oceans International *World's First 3D Printed Reef*, Media Release (29 October 2012). Available from: http://www.sustainable-oceans.com.au/images/stories/Media_releases/SOI_Worlds_FIRST_3D_printed_reef_MEDIA_RELEASE_2012.pdf

Michael Weinberg *What's the Deal with Copyright and 3D Printing?* (29 January 2013). Available from: http://www.publicknowledge.org/Copyright-3DPrinting

INDEX